PREFACE

THE compilation of any anthology is an ungrateful task ; and it is especially ungrateful when personal taste is the chief ground for selection. This symposium of French novelists is bound to disappoint many. Readers will cry, " Where is this one, where is that ? " And the compiler's answer will be that the novelists here included have been chosen for two reasons. First because their work seems to her to attain most fully to that aim of all great novels defined by no less a novelist than Maurice Barrès as the elevating and broadening of the mind and heart. *Quelque conception que l'on ait du roman*, he writes, *le but reste toujours le même, c'est d'élargir l'âme.* Secondly these novelists have been chosen because in their works are reflected most clearly the various tendencies of life and thought in France in the years which immediately preceded the War.

The novels of Marcelle Tinayre and of the Tharauds, for example, represent that purely artistic aspiration which is never absent from French literature. The great novel of Romain Rolland, "that admirable painter of disorder," as he has been called, represents what has been described as *l'école de la vie.* René Boylesve's novels are touched with the spirit of the Catholic and classical revival, which was a marked feature of France on the eve of the War. Pierre Mille's work illustrates at once the persistence of the intellectualism of Voltaire and of Renan, and the vigour of that energy which is so striking a characteristic of Young France. The popularity of Jean Aicard's picaresque novels proves that in spite of a classical renaissance, romanticism is not dead in France.

In this series as in the earlier volume the bibliographies at the beginnings of chapters are not restricted to works of fiction. To

FRENCH NOVELISTS OF TO-DAY
SECOND SERIES

MARCELLE TINAYRE
From a painting by De la Perche

FRENCH NOVELISTS OF TO-DAY

BY WINIFRED (WHALE) STEPHENS

SECOND SERIES

Essay Index Reprint Series

BOOKS FOR LIBRARIES PRESS
FREEPORT, NEW YORK

First Published 1915
Reprinted 1968

LIBRARY OF CONGRESS CATALOG CARD NUMBER:
68-20339

PRINTED IN THE UNITED STATES OF AMERICA

avoid confusion the titles of novels are printed in larger type.

The author is glad to take this opportunity of thanking those novelists who have kindly aided her in drawing up the bibliographical lists and who have generously placed their works at her disposal.

WINIFRED STEPHENS.

LONDON, 1915.

CONTENTS

LIST OF ILLUSTRATIONS

FRENCH NOVELISTS OF TO-DAY

INTRODUCTION

THE FRENCH NOVEL ON THE EVE OF THE WAR

To all previous events, however recent, the War lends a curious remoteness. Things that happened to us as individuals only last summer seem now as if they had befallen some one else. Recent national events appear as if they had taken place in some dimly distant epoch of time or in another universe. Never perhaps within the memory of man has so insuperable a barrier been erected between one period and another as that which was raised on July 28, 1914, when Austria declared war against Servia. Since then all things have become new. Those therefore who, amidst the emotions and activities of war-time, have leisure and inclination for looking backward, may now occupy a superb vantage-point, whence to view the period which has definitely and finally closed.

Consequently a survey of French fiction on the eve of the War needs no apology. Just now we are all interested in France, once "our sweet enemy" now our dear ally. And if we would know what France was thinking on the eve of the War we must read French fiction; for there is no clearer and more faithful mirror of French life and thought than the French novel. Here we find an explanation of that remarkable change which, during the last fifteen years, has been coming over the French spirit, and of those new characteristics—hardiness, tenacity, endurance, and readiness to submit to discipline—which the War is revealing. The French novels produced since the beginning of the century show that France, like the rest of Western Europe, has been experiencing a revolt against intellectualism; that in French writers there has been a tendency to return to authority—to evince a preference for instinctive rather than rational methods, to insist that man is after all only a little bit reasonable, that reason plays a very minor part in his life; and even to minimise that minor part. "What a little thing upon the surface of ourselves is intelligence!" exclaimed the novelist, M. Maurice Barrès, whose works are full of these tendencies. Those who are in any degree acquainted with the elder generation of contemporary French writers and thinkers will readily perceive that the appearance of such tendencies constituted a veritable revolution, a complete *volte-face*. They involved the rejection of those eighteenth century ideas still held by the elder writers of modern France—by the prince of intellectuals, M. Anatole France, by M. J. H. Rosny, by M. Remy de Gourmont, and many others. The appearance of these tendencies seemed to indicate that Young France was stiffening her neck against the gospel of Voltaire and bowing it to receive the yoke of Bossuet, that she was revolting against the scepticism of her fathers and returning to the dogmatism of her great-grandfathers, that, in a word, while the elder generation doubted everything, the younger generation believed everything. Young France on the eve of the War was with all her soul rejecting *der Geist der stets verneint*.

To appreciate the completeness of this change one has only to compare the chief characters in famous novels of this century—of *Jean Christophe*, for example—with those of equally famous novels produced only twenty years ago, such as *Cruelle Enigme* or *Mensonges* of Bourget. Take the young Hubert Liauran in *Cruelle Enigme*, take the young René Vinci in *Mensonges*, and compare their sad philosophy of life with the unquestioning optimism of young Georges Jeannin in *La Nouvelle Journée*, the last volume of *Jean Christophe*. Or compare the elder and the younger generation as they are represented in the pages of *Jean Christophe*. Compare the optimism of Georges Jeannin with the pessimism of his father Olivier, Christophe's bosom friend. Olivier is typical of the elder generation; he is a sceptic, an ironist, a psychologist, and so analytical as to be frequently morbid. Olivier's son, Georges, is totally unlike his father. "I can't think whom you resemble," his mother used to say. "Certainly neither me nor your father." From the teachers who had inspired Olivier, Georges turned away with disgust. Tolstoy he condemned as a mere nihilist, Ibsen as a proud destroyer, Nietzsche as a raving madman, Renan and

Anatole France as dilettanti whose irony lacks distinction and whose laughter is empty of merriment. While Olivier was content to leave certain problems unsolved, Georges pined for certainty in all things ; and in order to obtain it he was prepared to accord to authority that submission which his father had ever proudly denied. *Malheur au vague, mieux vaut le faux* might have been his motto. Consumed with this longing for certitude, desiring discipline, respecting authority, Georges and his young friends are perpetually forming themselves into societies and laying down rules and principles. Georges fails to understand why his father's old friend, Christophe, has never felt the need of joining some camp.

"A camp!" cried Christophe, "why should one shut oneself up in a camp. Isn't it much better outside. I am surprised that you, an out-of-doors man, should want to shut yourself up!"

"Ah, it is not the same thing for the body as for the soul," replied Georges. "The mind needs certitude. It needs to think with others, it needs to adopt principles admitted by the mass of mankind at a given period.

How I envy those who lived in classic times. My friends are right when they want to restore those good old days."

"Poor fool," cried Christophe, "what has made you so chicken-hearted?"

"I am not chicken-hearted," Georges indignantly protested. "Neither are any of us."

"You must be," said Christophe, "if you are so afraid of yourselves. What! you need an order, a rule, and yet you are so incapable of finding one for yourselves that you must needs hang on to your great grandmother's apron strings! Good heavens! Can't you walk alone?"

"We must take root, *s'enraciner*," said Georges, proud to repeat one of the catchwords of the day.

"But do trees need to be in pots in order to take root? The earth's there, free to every one. Strike your roots deep into it. Find your own laws. Look within you."

"I haven't the time," said Georges.

Here is one of the reasons for the young Frenchman's reversion to authority, for his passion for herding together in societies. In the rush of modern existence he had no time to discover for himself the certainty for which he craved. In the turmoil of a mechanical age, Young France was in no danger of suffering from the malady of too much thinking. Hurrying to football, whirling in a motor-car, soaring in an aeroplane, what time had she for that systematic thought which was the basis of French rationalism—what time for "those deliberate formulæ, syllogisms and classifications which were the basis of French thought and out of which were evolved ideals, the attempted realisation whereof sometimes altered the history of the world?"

In the hurry and scurry of modern life, in the present mania for sport, we may find some explanation of the tendencies which have been revealing themselves in Young France. Never had the physical activity of France been so great as on the eve of the War. The gospel of Energy preached by M. Barrès in his novels grouped under the title of *Energie Nationale* had indeed fallen upon fruitful ground. "Intoxicated with the sense of his muscular vigour, he would have set out to conquer the stars," wrote a novelist of his hero. The same remark might apply to the majority of young Frenchmen in the trenches to-day.

This type of young Frenchman, an athlete *mens sana in corpore sano*, is the hero of M. André Lichtenberger's last novel, *Le Sang Nouveau*. This book depicts the striking contrast which exists in France between the three generations: to-day, represented by the hero, Max; yesterday, by the father of Max, Geoffrey; and the day before yesterday, by the grandfather of Max, Jean Jacques Dailliot. Geoffrey, the father, stands in the middle, isolated, totally incapable of understanding either the ideals of his son, or his own father's vague sympathy with his grandson's interests and ambitions.

In a conversation, which should be read by all who wish to understand France on the eve of the War, Jean Jacques Dailliot endeavours to dispel some of the prejudices which obscure his son Geoffrey's vision.

"You must know, my son," says Jean Jacques, the scientist, to Geoffrey, who is a man of business, "that it is very difficult to decipher the soul of the generation which is rising behind us and gradually pushing us into the grave. Did you ever realize how it grieved me a quarter of a century ago to renounce my hope of associating you in my life's work, and how it cut me to the heart to see you restricting your activities to business and local politics? Science then seemed to hold out hopes not merely of a renaissance in France, but of universal progress and of an approaching era in which justice and prosperity should reign. That you should forsake me then seemed like a desertion, or, if you will, like a fall. . . . I was unjust, and after a time I realized it; and I never reproached you with the career that you had chosen."

With deep feeling Geoffrey replied:

"I trust that, though I may have failed to express it, you have felt my gratitude. But you must admit that my ambitions, though not identical with yours and though not altogether realized, were nevertheless neither trivial nor despicable. To enrich my country and the family I had founded by my industry, and to consecrate to the triumph of democracy the surplus of my energy, was, you must confess, no mean ideal. Let Max declare one which is as worthy, and joyfully will I imitate that abnegation of which you have set me the example. . . . But I wait and see no sign of it."

"Perhaps because you are blind . . . because we are both blind."

The man of business looked questioningly at his father.

"What do you mean ?"

"This."

For a moment the old man reflected. Then he continued :

"I shall make you smile. My conversion dates from the football match or rather from the series of impressions it made upon me, which have, not without difficulty, cast the scales from my eyes. You must know, my son, that in our day there exist two Frances. One is ours, the France which you see ; but this France is disappearing. It guides the State, it acts through our governing bodies, it expresses itself in our literature and in our newspapers. A consuming thirst for perfection, a feverish and hypercritical intellectualism—these are its characteristics. And while the dwellers in this France, ranged beneath rival standards, are ceaselessly fighting against one another, behind them ruins are being heaped up in stagnant waters.

"Side by side with this France, almost beyond it, there is another France growing up. At present it has no official organ. It is barely conscious of itself. But here and there one may feel its heart beating—in some new review or bit of a newspaper article, in some letter from a young lieutenant stationed in Morocco or Ouadaï, in some student's manifestation. These acts and declarations are disconcerting, and they appear incoherent. This new France has its training-ground: it is the world of sport in which it develops its muscles and strengthens its will."

To sport, in which Young France before the War was so passionately engaging, Lichtenberger looked for the regeneration of his country. First because it was fostering in French youth a spirit of conflict, a desire for discipline, a longing for victory. Secondly, because it conduced, so he said, to purity of life—Lichtenberger was a firm believer in the high ethical influence of the football-field. He, like his hero, Jean Jacques, had been converted to the gospel of athletics by a football match. "Not only," he writes, "does it broaden the chest and develop the muscles, it fortifies the soul, it inculcates the virtues of self-discipline, courage, sang-froid, abnegation, and solidarity." Lichtenberger, little dreaming how soon France was to demand precisely these virtues from her sons, expected much from football. Other novelists, notably M. Romain Rolland, the development of so much muscular energy filled with alarm. They were inclined to hold it responsible for that intellectual indolence which to them seemed to be carrying France into the arms of reaction!

In three distinct, though closely interrelated, departments of thought this reaction declared itself: in political speculation, in religion and in more abstract philosophy. In political speculation, monarchism and nationalism seemed to be gaining ground, and close upon their heels ran anti-Semitism, militarism, and a kind of aggressive imperialism, which was new in the France of that day, although its prototype might be discovered during the Revolution. Monarchism and nationalism were respectively associated with the work of an eminent writer: monarchism with Charles Maurras, nationalism with Maurice Barrès, both household names in

France though in England hitherto little known.

These two reactionary writers exercised a profound influence over French youth largely through their command of a masterly style. The easy security of the style of Maurras entitles him to rank with Anatole France as one of the greatest masters of modern French. In literary criticism he has been truly described as the most brilliant critic of pure letters in French since Sainte-Beuve. Unhappily he has of late years seen fit to forsake letters for politics; and his virulent monarchism and anti-Semitism warp even those critical articles which now and again he contributes to the newspaper *l'Action Française*. Thus in a recent review of M. Pierre Champion's noble *Life of Villon*,[1] M. Maurras devoted nearly the whole of his article to a bitter and totally irrelevant attack, inspired entirely by his Israelitish origin, on that brilliant essayist, the late Marcel Schwob, whose work on Villon M. Champion has continued.

Barrès,[2] too, is a stylist of great charm and

[1] *François Villon, Sa Vie et Son Temps*. 2 vols. Paris. Honoré Champion.

[2] For the early novels of Barrès see the present writer's *French Novelists of To-day* (1st series).

power. It is difficult to attach to him any one literary label. Some have called him "the imperturbable romantic," yet in his novel *Colette Baudoche* he has produced a treasure of classicism. To cite a recent critic, "there is no living writer like M. Barrès! Subtle, brilliant, delicate, violent, he turns up every time in a different place from that where we expected to find him."

This is an age of hero-worship in France. Maurice Barrès inaugurated it with a glorification of Taine and Napoleon in his novel *les Déracinés*, published in 1897. Romain Rolland in the new century has followed suit in his three masterpieces of biography—his *Beethoven*, his *Michael Angelo*, and his *Tolstoy*. For a number of young Frenchmen on the eve of the War Charles Maurras was almost as great a hero as Taine was for Barrès thirty years ago, or as Tolstoy was for Romain Rolland twenty years ago. The personal charm of M. Maurras, his scholarship, his disinterestedness, the simplicity almost amounting to asceticism of his private life, made a strong appeal to young Frenchmen and caused them to excuse too easily the violence of his hatreds and the truculence of his attacks on his opponents. M. Maurras is a devout admirer of the classic age of French literature and French history. He is indeed a Frenchman of *le Grand Siècle* born out of due time. His views on society, on the Republic, and on the Church he has expressed in numerous works, which are all widely read. The chief perhaps are *Trois Idées Politiques, Chateaubriand, Michelet, Sainte-Beuve ; l'Enquête sur la Monarchie ; Kiel et Tanger* and *la Politique Religieuse.*

It was Maurras who, in 1905, founded the Royalist Society known as l'Action Française. Every member of this society is required to sign a declaration closing with the words : *je m'associe à l'œuvre de la restauration monarchique, je m'engage à la servir par tous les moyens. Par tous les moyens* includes violence when necessary. The members of l'Action Française, which is not ostensibly a Catholic society, for it includes many freethinkers, among whom is Maurras himself, unblushingly encouraged and justified the violence which attended the taking of the inventories of church property, those stormy scenes reproduced with such vividness in the pages of M. Bourget's *l'Emigré.* Maurras is also the dominating spirit of the newspaper *l'Action Française.* To its columns he subscribes, side by side with articles of the most finished and accomplished literary criticism, panegyrics of royalty and attacks on the French Republic and all its works.[1] These attacks are too often expressed in scurrilous language interlarded with invective of the most vitriolic order. When unsullied by abuse the articles of Maurras are couched in a lucid, emphatic, yet dignified French prose, the style of which one cannot refrain from admiring, though with the matter one may profoundly disagree.

Maurras as well as an anti-republican is an anti-democrat and an anti-romanticist. He prides himself on taking large views of life. His conception of the universe he proudly asserts to be that of Aristotle, Dante, and Bossuet. This was the grand conception, he maintains, which dominated before those miserable Romanticists Rousseau and his school came to give undue prominence to the individual and to glorify under the name of Justice or Liberty or Progress one single

[1] Even in war-time, when other controversialists are silent, M. Maurras finds it difficult to control his waspish pen; and his attitude towards the present Government is one of thinly veiled hostility.

aspiration. Those Romanticists, says Maurras, were blinded by passion; they misread the face of the Universe. It remains for Maurras to read it aright and to reinstate reason in her sovereign sway.

Maurras would sacrifice everything to what he calls the integrity of society and to the harmonious working of the social order. Thus, on the eve of the 1914 elections we find him writing in *l'Action Française*: "Le seul souverain c'est le bien public, non l'opinion qu'en peut avoir majorité ou minorité. Chez nous, pour des raisons liées au territoire de nos races, le bien public s'incarne dans la royauté. Elle a fait la France, tous les autres gouvernements n'ont contribué, jamais, qu'à la défaire. Le gouvernement royal est le seul normal." For Maurras *le bien public*, as he calls it, is more important than the rights of any single individual—we presume even than the rights of M. Maurras himself—certainly than the rights of a persecuted Jew, Alfred Dreyfus. Maurras, as we might expect, has always been bitterly anti-Dreyfusard. It was during the crisis of l'Affaire Dreyfus that Maurras founded the newspaper *l'Action Française*, which long kept l'Affaire alive. Largely owing to Maurras and *l'Action Française* l'Affaire was still, on the eve of the War, a living force in French society. It would be difficult to exaggerate the importance of the part played by l'Affaire in the history of modern French literature. Nearly all the leading French writers passionately espoused either one side or the other. Zola did not live to introduce it into his novels. But his *Letters* on l'Affaire rank among his masterpieces. Anatole France in *l'Histoire Contemporaine* and in *Crainquebille* produced some of his most significant work, so also on the other side did M. Barrès in his *Scènes et Doctrines du Nationalisme*.

In the movement of French thought this great law-suit represents much more than the question of the guilt or innocence of an officer in the French army accused of selling military information to the foreigner. L'Affaire represents the conflict between two ideas neither of them contemptible. The real question at issue during the great national crisis was this: is it right at all times and under all circumstances to proclaim the truth? The anti-Dreyfusards asserted that it is not. They maintained that if the proclamation of the truth endangers the security of society, then the truth should not be told. The Dreyfusards asserted that in all times, under all circumstances, whatever the cost, the truth should be told.

This problem is an old one and a difficult. The pardon and rehabilitation of Dreyfus have not solved it. And so the conflict between Dreyfusards and anti-Dreyfusards continued. To see it you had only to take up any issue of *l'Action Française*. Constantly there appeared in this paper a calendar recalling from the anti-Dreyfus point of view the chief events of l'Affaire. On the other side the late M. Charles Péguy,[1] *conteur*, poet and journalist, kept l'Affaire alive in the interesting pages of the periodical *Les Cahiers de la Quinzaine*, which he founded and edited.

[1] The heroism with which Péguy had defended the cause of Dreyfus he carried into the War. How completely he won the esteem of the soldiers whom he commanded as lieutenant is testified by one of them who wrote of him: "He was insensible to fatigue, brave under fire, living like the rest of us, *i.e.* eating one day out of three, ever without a murmur, and ever young in spite of his age." Always in the post of danger, Péguy met with his death, in the Battle of the Marne, when leading his men to capture a German position, on September 5, 1914.

To save France from destruction Maurras believed it necessary to restore the rule of King and Pope. For in M. Maurras and in M. Barrès also, as we shall see later, the two tides of political and Catholic reaction meet. Yet the droll part of it is that neither Maurras nor Barrès is a Catholic. Far from it, Maurras is an avowed atheist, Barrès is an agnostic. To an English mind it seems almost inconceivable that an avowed atheist should so strenuously advocate Catholicism as M. Maurras has done in his book *La Politique Religieuse.* Here we find his hatred of Jerusalem and Geneva inducing him, as he expresses it, to kneel reverently before " the ancient and holy maternal figure of historical Catholicism." He is apparently oblivious of the fact that even Catholicism owes its existence to a Jew. With curious inconsistence he hails the Church as the ark of salvation of society, and the Noah of that ark he declares to be " the sovereign pontiff who, clothed in white raiment, sits upon the summit of the Catholic system " as " the demiurgos of universal civilization." While the works of M. Maurras were widely read and while they contributed all along the line to strengthen reaction, there appeared little danger of his monarchical views being widely accepted. Although his ideas are implicit in much French fiction there is, as far as I know, only one novel, M. Bourget's *l'Emigré*, which definitely advocates the restoration of *l'Ancien Régime.*

More practical and more dangerous from the progressive point of view than the monarchicism of M. Maurras are the nationalist ideas of the republican, M. Maurice Barrès. In view of the fact that for more than forty years France has been a Republic, M. Barrès, who is a traditionalist, cannot help being a republican. However he may admire monarchy—and he does admire it—M. Barrès realizes that any attempt to restore that form of government in France must end in failure. *Cultivez vos morts* is his doctrine. In other words, continue in the footsteps of your ancestors, but in this case of your immediate ancestors only. The nationalism of M. Barrès has evolved out of regionism and traditionism. The present writer in the first volume of this series has shown how these two closely interrelated theories gradually took form in the early novels of M. Barrès.

In one of these, *l'Œil des Barbares*, the author, like Pater in the famous conclusion of his *Renaissance*, entrenched himself in the isolation of perfect egoism, which he calls *le culte du moi*. In a second novel, *l'Homme Libre*, and in *le Jardine de Bérénice*, the most artistic of his works, he teaches—all M. Barrès' works are didactic—that *le culte du moi* is not enough, that no man can be healthy without a certain *sociabilité*. It is this vague idea of *sociabilité* which materializes into regionism and traditionism. "Every region," writes Barrès, "presents an idea, and that idea one must allow to soak into one's being." His own native region is Lorraine. The spirit of Lorraine pervades all his books. In *Les Déracinées* four youths of Lorraine, who leave their native province to settle in Paris, come to no good, three of them at least, because they have isolated themselves from their native atmosphere, because they have been false to the principle of regionism. Traditionism is harmony with the spirit of one's ancestors. "A Catholic," writes M. Barrès, "founds his patriotism on his religion." But he who cannot accept the supernatural must bring his piety down from heaven to earth, to the earth wherein repose his dead. If we would attain to the full measure of our being, if we would accept in its fulness the Gospel of Energy which M. Barrès preaches, then we must cultivate all that is racial within us. " In us all," he continues, " are survivals, *il y a des survivances, qui, bien dégagés nous donneraient du style*." Thus M. Barrès, when he visits Brittany, makes pilgrimages to certain sites which are most in accord with the spirit of his Lotharingian origin. He avoids the Forest of Broceliande as being too Celtic. But he takes care that his due feet do not fail to tread the hallowed ground of *Les Rochers*, once the abode of that typical Frenchwoman, Madame de Sévigné, and Combourg, where in boyhood dwelt Chateaubriand, the apostle of that romanticism which M. Barrès believes to be the dominant feature in the spirit of his native Lorraine.

Regionism and traditionism lead to nationalism. What is nationalism ? M. France, the arch enemy of nationalism, in his Preface to the speeches of M. Combes, thus describes the rise of this movement :

" The anti-Semites were soon joined by a numerous party, *le parti noir*, who in salon and suburb, in town and country, spread abroad alarming reports, spoke vaguely of plots and of treasons, stirred up the patriotism of the people by making them tremble for their safety, by inspiring them with wrath and with fear. As yet this party took care not to appear in the open. It worked in the shadow—a vague influence—not unlike that exercised by the mailed monks of the League. But when it had rallied all the forces of the counter-revolutions and attracted the innumerable malcontents of the Republic, when in short it had raised all that human dust which it is possible for a gust of public opinion to raise, then it uplifted its immense countenance and assumed the name of nationalism."

In a very different spirit has nationalism been described by the captain of the movement, M. Barrès, in a book entitled *Scènes et Doctrines du Nationalisme* (1902). It is significant that this book was the outcome of l'Affaire Dreyfus; for the events of that great national crisis caused the ideas M. Barrès calls nationalism to materialize in his mind. Nationalism is in brief the carrying of racialism to its extreme limit, the raising high of the barriers of race and nationality against all foreign influence, whether it come from within the nation, from Jews and others settled in the country, or from without, from foreigners, especially Germans on the frontier. Nationalism before the War involved anti-Semitism. It does not now involve it; for side by side and arm in arm Catholic priests and Jewish rabbis go forth to the trenches. One of the root principles of nationalism was *La Revanche.* Barrès, in his novel *Les Amitiés Françaises,*[1] describes the education of a little French boy, Philip, in the principles of nationalism. Philip's father takes his son to the battlefields of Lorraine where the French suffered defeat during the war of 1870. He conducts Philip to the battlefield of Worth and there he presents him with the humiliating picture of a Prussian officer spitting in the face of his French prisoner. "Philip," says his father, "I give you this tradition. Here more plainly than in any book you will see the barrier that separates France from Germany." The eternal incompatibility of the German and French

[1] Not that Barrès ever advocated declaring war against Germany. All that he urged was that France should prepare for the German attack, which, he believed, was bound to come.

temperaments was a favourite theme with M. Barrès as it was with many other French novelists. M. Barrès has developed it again in *Colette Baudoche*, M. Paul Margueritte in *Les Frontières du Cœur*, and M. René Bazin in *Les Oberlé*.[1]

Another form of nationalism declared itself in the numerous colonial and maritime novels which were being written in France before the War. Pierre Loti has a disciple and a very able one in Claude Farrère, the author of *La Bataille*, *l'Homme qui assassina* and *Thomas l'Agnelet, Gentilhomme de Fortune*. But there is a difference between Farrère and his master which is characteristic of the new spirit, for the younger writer has none of that melancholy which sheds a poetic charm like the mist of an autumn day over the pages of *Mon Frère Yves*, *Pêcheurs d'Islande* and *Madame Chrysanthème*. The novels of Farrère glow with the bright hopefulness of springtime, with the glad confidence of youth.

The energy of the new spirit also gave rise to a whole crop of colonial novels—those of Henry Daguerche for example—and to a

[1] Other Alsatian novels are: Acker's *Les Exilés* and Oncle Hansi's *Mon Village*.

great appreciation of Rudyard Kipling in France. Mr. Kipling has an able imitator in M. Pierre Mille, who was once London correspondent of *Le Temps*. Despite the very pronounced Gallicism of M. Mille, his stories are being translated into English.

It was in keeping with the militarism of the new spirit that at least two well-known novelists were soldiers, M. Emile Nolly, whose remarkable story, *le Conquérant*, is now (February 1915) appearing in *La Revue de Paris*, and M. Ernest Psichari, the grandson of the great Renan. M. Psichari's recent heroic death renders it difficult to write frankly of his work as a novelist, especially of his manifesto of militarism, *l'Appel des Armes*. The doctrine he advocated with such impassioned fervour the author has now sealed with the last and greatest sacrifice a man can make. To his life history, which is typical of the new spirit dawning in France before the War, his death imparts a striking unity. His own story he has related in his book, *Terres de Soleil et Sommeil*, which appeared in 1908. Here he tells of his childhood in his Paris home and his visits to the Breton village, where he recalls seeing his grandfather, "weighed down with thoughts and with genius," strolling through the pine woods, then of his university studies, and finally of the great awakening which came to him in his African travels. Returning home to write his Sorbonne thesis on the decay of idealism he was haunted by visions of the Dark Continent until, shaking the dust of schools and colleges from his feet, he returned to Africa as a lieutenant of colonial artillery. The rare leisure of a military life he employed in writing his novel, *l'Appel des Armes*, which he completed in the Sahara in 1912. This book he dedicated to Charles Péguy. To Péguy and to Psichari was it given to receive in the Battle of the Marne an answer to that prayer which the author of *l'Appel des Armes* puts into the mouth of his hero, Maurice Vincent, "Grant me, O Lord God, to die in some great victory."

The fact that both these writers may be numbered among *les Grands Convertis* is only one of many proofs that a Catholic Revival had set in in France before the War. But it was a movement restricted to the well-to-do and cultured classes.

More than once in the pages of his novel,

La Révolte des Anges, this fashionableness of religion provoked the irony of Anatole France :

" L'esprit public s'améliorait," he writes. " Les Jacobins, les franc-maçons, les blocards étaient partout hormis. L'élite donnait le bon exemple. L'Académie française était bien pensante. Les écoles chrétiennes se multipliaient. La jeunesse du Quartier Latin se soumettait à l'Eglise et l'École Normale exhalait les parfums du séminaire. La croix triomphait."

Among the people, however, rationalism still reigned. Even a Catholic admitted that the workshop continued closed against the Church. Those who returned to the rites and sacraments of Catholicism were the scholars at lycées and the students at universities. " La foi a ses vicissitudes," to quote again from *La Révolte des Anges*. " Sous l'ancien régime, le peuple était croyant ; la noblesse ne l'était pas, ni la bourgeoisie lettrée. Sous le premier Empire, l'armée du haut en bas était fort impie. Aujourd'hui, le peuple ne croit à rien. La bourgeoisie veut croire et y réussit quelquefois." The Frenchman of the professional class a generation ago never entered a church from his first Communion to his funeral, except perhaps on his wedding day and at the baptism of his children. Among the cultured youths of modern France this is far from being the case now. Young Frenchmen go to church. L'Association Catholique de la Jeune France, which is only one of many societies for French youths, numbers one hundred and twenty thousand members, all between the ages of fifteen and thirty, and most of them weekly communicants.

In family life the French are always intensely conservative. Even rationalist Frenchmen have often been pleased for their women folk to continue Catholic. A certain Catholic atmosphere has never vanished from many rationalist homes. Only the other day a French agnostic of the Quartier Latin told me that at the fête of St. Geneviève he always places a candle on the altar of St. Etienne-du-Mont. It was his parents' church, he had been baptised there, and this act of his seemed a deed of filial piety. An Englishwoman of my acquaintance, who went as paying guest into a Parisian family, told me her hostess met her on the threshold with the words uttered rather nervously: "I think I ought to tell you that we are all freethinkers here: I am a freethinker, my husband is a freethinker, and my son is a freethinker." My friend received this announcement with an equanimity which was somewhat disturbed when, on entering her room, she found a crucifix hanging over her bed.

Into a soil wherein still linger so many superstitions of the past have fallen the seeds of new influences—Barrèsian traditionism, a weakness for mysticism and an anti-rationalist philosophy. In such a soil these tendencies have easily taken root and readily sprung up to bear the fruit of a Catholic revival. In the history of this revival from its beginning at the verge of the nineties down to the present day, the novel has played a significant part. Two eminent novelists, Huysmanns and Bourget, were among the earliest *Grands Convertis*. Indeed the rise of the psychological novel, of which Bourget was such a distinguished exponent, may be regarded as the prelude to the Catholic Revival.

In the appearance of Zola's *La Terre* in 1887, realism reached its high-water mark. Then almost immediately the tide of realism began to ebb. *La Terre*, the most completely realistic of all Zola's novels, turned even his ardent admirers against him. Five of them drew up a manifesto accusing him of having in this novel descended *au fond de l'immondice*. From a work like Zola's, from which the soul of man was excluded, Young France of the late eighties turned with disgust. Among Zola's most faithful disciples had been the young novelist, Edouard Rod. Yet even he, in his preface to *Les Trois Cœurs*, a novel which appeared in 1890, three years after *La Terre*, wrote of himself and his fellow disciples that in conviction they might be realists, in temperament they never were. "We had aspirations," he wrote, "that could never be satisfied by realism, which was essentially self-satisfied, narrow and materialist, more curious about manners than about character, about things than about souls: we were, and we were becoming more and more restless, idealist, in love with the infinite, caring little for manners, in everything always seeking man." M. Bourget was not then an idealist like Rod. But in his early novels, *Une Cruelle Enigme*, *un Crime d'Amour* and *Mensonges* it was essentially with the mental and moral aspect of man's nature that he was concerned. These novels mark the beginning of a new movement in literature, a revolt against realism. This literary revolt was being encouraged in philosophy by the anti-materialistic movement led by Guyau, Boutroux and Bergson. Renan had written in *l'Avenir de la Science*: "*je jouerais cent fois ma vie et par conséquent mon salut éternel pour la vérité scientifique de la thèse rationaliste.*" But already when that book appeared, in 1890, philosophers were beginning to lose faith in science. They were ceasing to look to science for the solution of ultimate problems. Science herself was assuming a more modest position than of old. She was no longer claiming to explain phenomena themselves so much as to state their relations to one another. Philosophers, like Guyau, Boutroux, Bergson and William James, whose influence in France has been considerable, were attaching less importance to the part played by intelligence in the scheme of things, they were assigning more prominence than their predecessors had given to instinct and to intuition; they were beginning to show sympathy with all forms of religion; they were beginning to revel in those mysteries of the Unknowable and the Inexplicable from which their predecessors had stood aloof.

This growing dissatisfaction with rationalism Paul Bourget powerfully expressed in his *Essais de Psychologie Contemporaine,* which appeared in 1883. Against this philosophy, six years later in his novel *Le Disciple,* he brought a serious indictment ; for here he represented it as responsible for the vicious experiment committed by the hero of the novel. The book is indeed the manifesto of the new school, the school of mysticism as opposed to that of rationalism. In his preface Bourget called upon the youth of France to believe in the existence of a soul and of a future life. Bourget was not then a Catholic, but that he was rapidly moving in that direction was proved by his next novel of note, *La Terre Promise,* while *l'Etape,* published ten years after *Le Disciple,* proved that Bourget had definitely committed himself heart and soul to the cause of reaction. In *l'Etape* he appears as traditionalist, Catholic and monarchist. Bourget is only one of many examples that might be cited to prove that the new anti-rationalist philosophy is but a stepping-stone to Catholicism. M. Charles Péguy was another case in point. M. Barrès will furnish yet another example when at length he decides to enter that Church, whither his anti-rationalism and his traditionalist principles rapidly impel him.

Writing in the *Mercure de France* on November 1, 1910, M. Remy de Gourmont pointed out how James and Professor Bergson have been unconsciously working for Christianity. Indeed, M. Bergson's philosophy has been said to have done more to open church doors than any movement of thought since Aristotelianism. In an inquiry which two French writers, M. Henri Massis and M. Alfred de Tarde, have recently been conducting into the opinions of Young France,[1] they discover that most young French Catholic converts ascribe their conversion either to the influence of M. Bergson or to that of M. Barrès, or sometimes to the influence of both. "I should have been absolutely irreligious if I had never studied philosophy," writes one of Bergson's disciples. "All the most vital principles of Bergson's philosophy may be discovered in

[1] See their book, *Les Jeunes Gens d'Aujourd'hui*.

theological teaching of all ages," writes another. While a third confesses that in *l'Evolution Créatrice* he felt God on every page.

The stream of the modern Catholic Revival, like that of all French Catholic thought for at least three centuries, flows in two main currents, one dogmatic, constructive, classical, the other mystic, liberal, romantic. The former to-day is dominated by the traditionism of Barrès, the latter by the Vitalism—as we in England call it—of Bergson. Of the first M. Bourget is the typical representative, uncompromisingly reactionary and ultramontane, descending from Bossuet, through Bonald and de Maistre. Of the latter, M. Charles Péguy was typical. He derived from St. François de Sales through Fénelon and Lamennais. In temperament M. Péguy was a mystic. His love of liberty inclined him to Gallicanism. His politics were Socialist. His most profoundly religious works are his poems, *les Mystères de Jeanne d'Arc* and *Ève*.[1]

In the realm of fiction the first of the

[1] Two minor currents of Catholicism are Modernism and the liberal Catholicism of M. Marc Sangnier, whose society le Sillon has recently been dissolved by the Pope.

Catholic tendencies is represented by M. Bourget's three Catholic novels, *l'Etape, un Divorce,* and *l'Emigré,* the second by those numerous mystic novels which enjoyed a great vogue in France on the eve of the War. Figuring first among novels of Catholic mysticism it is surprising to find a work by the agnostic Barrès, *La Colline Inspirée,* which is perhaps the most profound and subtly psychological study M. Barrès has yet given us. Another beautifully written mystical novel is *La Cité des Lampes* by Mlle. de Lévis, who writes under the pseudonym of Claude Silve, while yet another is *Laure* by Emile Clerment, a novel which only failed by two votes to win the Prix de l'Académie, which was assigned to *Jean Christophe. Jean Christophe* itself, in its ten volumes, includes pages touched with mysticism, though not Catholic mysticism. Another instance of the influence of the religious wave outside Catholic literature is a very remarkable novel, *La Porte Étroite,* by M. André Gide. It is perhaps somewhat surprising to find an author who ranks decidedly among the intellectuals treating such a subject. For in spite of the Catholic Revival there were still some intellectuals left in France. Though, after the numerous anti-intellectuals who have defiled before us in this chapter, after the battle we have witnessed between the black France and the red, we might doubt it. But yes, there were still many who had not bowed the knee to the Baal of positive affirmation. many who, with that sad but strong patience, which characterized the great thinkers of an elder generation, were content to wait for a solution of life's problems, who were even strong enough to admit that the solution may never appear, that the finite may ever be incapable of grasping the infinite. Over this band of intellectualists the subtle irony, the tender pity, the clear, august, classic style of Anatole France raised him supreme. M. Jean Rosny and M. Remi de Gourmont were other elder writers who nobly maintained the tradition of Voltaire and of Renan. Among the younger men were M. André Gide, whom we have already mentioned, and the ardent adversary of Bergson, M. Julien Benda, whose powerful novel, *l'Ordination*, was much discussed. The intellectuals in France were still a great power. In the opinion of many they represented the main current of French thought. But it was not a new current. It was rather one which had long vivified that old France which we love, not the black France or the red, but the golden France, shedding its rays of sunlight on the whole world of thought, representing all that is noblest, healthiest and most sane in the genius of a people who have so long been the intellectual leaders of the world. It is a current which has ever made for peace and unity.

For a word which has occurred over and over again in this chapter, the word Reaction, there are those, as we have said, who would substitute another, Renaissance. And far be it from me to deny that in certain respects even those tendencies of modern France, which to some seem reactionary, may bear within them the seeds of a new life. "That which seems to be dying is only beginning to be reborn" are words written upon the tombstone of the philosopher Guyau far away on the Mediterranean shore. "The history of survival," writes Tylor,[1] "has for the most part been a history of dwindling and decay. . . . But this is so far from being a law with-

[1] *Primitive Culture*, 4th ed., 1903, I., 136.

out exception that a narrow view of history may often seem to make it no law at all. For the stream of civilization winds and turns upon itself. . . . We may now and then trace on from the very turning point the change from passive survival into active revival."

> For each age is a dream that is dying,
> And one that is coming to birth.

MARCELLE TINAYRE

THE WORKS OF MARCELLE TINAYRE

1897. **Avant l'Amour.**
1898. **La Rançon.**
1899. **Hellé.**
1901. **L'Oiseau d'Orage.**
1902. **La Maison du Péché.**
1904. **La Vie Amoureuse de François Barbazanges.**
1905. **La Rebelle.**
1908. **L'Amour qui pleure.**
1909. Notes d'une Voyageuse en Turquie.
1909. **L'Ombre de l'Amour.**
1910. Une Journée de Port Royal.
1911. **La Douceur de Vivre.**
1913. **Madeleine au Miroir.**
1915. **Le Départ.**

MARCELLE TINAYRE, 1877

MADAME TINAYRE is a writer, the clear mirror of whose delicate art reflects the dawn of the new French spirit. She possesses, united to the average Frenchwoman's wake-mindedness and faculty for observation, the idealist's poetic soul. No great cause or noble sentiment ever failed to move her. Present-day problems keenly interest her; and artistically interwoven into the plots of her novels are such questions of the hour as the Near Eastern unrest, the principles of eugenists, the growing inevitability of war with Germany, and, finally, in her last novel, *le Départ*, the superb impulse with which, in the mobilization of August 1914, France rose to a man to repel the invader's attack. To those English readers who are in any way acquainted with Madame Tinayre's work she is too often known as the author of one book and one book only, *La Maison du Péché*. This novel is unquestionably her finest and her most aspiring work. But she has written other novels which no one interested in contemporary French fiction can afford to ignore. For in every one of them she appears as a consummate artist, a perfect mistress of the literary craft. The formlessness, now creeping over some modern French literature and unblushingly justified by certain eminent writers, Madame Tinayre abhors. That lightness and grace, that harmony and sense of proportion, so typically French, are never absent from a single page of her work.

For Marcelle Tinayre, *née* Chasteau, is French of the French. She was born in the heart of the French provinces, at the little town of Tulle, in Limousin, which she has described in more than one of her novels. In *Hellé* we may read how typically French was the landscape on which Marcelle's eyes first rested. In the pages of *Hellé* she recalls a hill-girt plain of heath and meadow, watered by a chestnut-shaded river, bearing its yellow waters past a little red-brick town dominated by a Norman belfry-tower. There must be something in the atmosphere of the legend-loving Limousin, which is especially favourable to the artistic genius, seeing that three of the most delicate literary artists of present-day France—Marcelle Tinayre, Jean and Jérôme Tharaud—are of Limousin origin. The exquisite artistry of Marcelle Tinayre's talent may also be accounted for by the fact that she belongs to a family adorned for generations by literary women. Her mother, Louise Chasteau, is a well-known novelist. Her grandmother was a poetess who corresponded with Lamartine. Still living in Madame Tinayre's memory is the recollection of her grandmother, of whom with all the delicate colouring of some ancient pastel she has sketched in her novels many a charming picture. In *Hellé* we recognize this graceful old lady in the white-haired, blue-eyed Madame Marboy, who was moved to tears even in old age by the poetry and romance of true love, who delighted to linger in churches, and who possessed all the superstitions and all the weaknesses of her sex. In *Madeleine au Miroir* we suspect that the same model served for Colette's mother-in-law, who, with her feet on a flowered woolwork carpet fashioned by her own hands in childhood, sat at her mahogany bureau writing delicately worded letters, by a window looking on to La Rue de La Temporalité in the provincial town of Roc-sur-Cère.

It was at her grandmother's knee that the little Marcelle learned to love the French romantic poets. Long before she could grasp their meaning, the melodious lines of Victor Hugo and Lamartine had engraved themselves on her memory. She herself lisped in numbers. When barely in her teens, under the influence of Pascal and Chateaubriand, she composed a long epic poem. Inspired by *Les Martyres*, she made her hero a pagan converted to Christianity by St. John in the island of Patmos. Missionary zeal carried the convert to remote Brittany. But there, while plucking Breton brands from the burning, like the hermit Paphnutius in the *Thaïs* of Anatole France, Marcelle Tinayre's hero lost his own soul through the fascinations of a beautiful heathen girl. The poem ends with the two lovers drowning themselves.

This favourite theme of the great French classic writers, the conflict between love and duty, between Christianity and Paganism, Marcelle Tinayre was later to develop in *La Maison du Péché*.

As she grew older Chateaubriand appealed less to Marcelle's admiration. But on her literary horizon Pascal's star never waned. Of all her literary gods he has continued one of the most ardently worshipped. It was her adoration of the Great Solitary that led Madame Tinayre to acquire that intimate knowledge of Port Royal and the Jansenist movement displayed in *La Maison du Péché*, and also in a charming little book, beautifully illustrated by her husband's engravings, entitled *Une Journée de Port Royal*.

In the matter of her works Madame Tinayre owes much to the great classic age of French literature. In manner she is true to her grandmother's teaching: she remains a romantic.

To Monsieur Tinayre, an engraver of Paris, Marcelle was married when she was but a child, and a very feminine child, for she is said to have wept on her wedding-day at not being allowed to go away in her wedding-frock.

Henceforth Madame Tinayre's home was in Paris. And, like every Frenchwoman, she was conquered at once by the attractions of that beautiful city. The spirit of Paris entered into her poetic soul. With delicate art and tender affection she has described its storied palaces, its domes and spires and its brilliant façades bathed in the soft morning mist, or glorified by the gorgeous hues of evening!

Yet, though she swiftly grew into a lover of Paris and a true Parisian with all the grace and sparkle of Parisian women, she always kept in her heart a place for her provincial home. Behind the complex culture of the townswoman, there is always something in Madame Tinayre's personality which suggests the simple charm of that romantic province, which she has so strikingly portrayed in her novel *l'Ombre de l'Amour.*

In Paris, Madame Tinayre, like so many literary and artistic souls, has always lived on the left bank of the Seine. Her flat, when I first called on her, was on the Boulevard Raspail. Later she moved to the Rue Cherche Midi. Now she occupies a charming little hotel, not far from the Avenue d'Orléans, in what she is pleased to call a truly provincial quarter of the capital. In a chapter of her recent book, *Madeleine au Miroir,* she describes her reluctant departure from the Rue Cherche Midi.

At least three other leading contemporary authors, Anatole France, Pierre Mille, and G. K. Chesterton, have written brilliantly and sympathetically on the same theme of house removal. But in poetical tenderness and romantic imagination neither of them has surpassed Madame Tinayre's farewell to her old home.

With regretful yearning she surveys the familiar rooms, the terraces and the courtyard with its Louis XV façade. All these things, affection invests with an old-world pathos. She recalls how the moonlight used to conjure phantoms out of the ancient stones. She remembers how when Paris was falling asleep, when the sounds of the great city were hushed and nought was heard save the occasional distant rumble of carriages, she would go out on to the terrace, where night, moonbeams and reverie mingled their enchantments and whence through the windows she would seem to see candles gleaming vaguely in the deserted rooms, a powdered head, a sweeping gown, and a flash of diamonds. A phantom violin quivered, and in the court-yard, round a pale, heatless fire, phantom lacqueys opened the doors of phantom coaches.

It is for her children's sake that Madame Tinayre has recently exchanged this old-world dwelling for her hotel near the Avenue d'Orléans. The Cherche-Midi flat had no modern conveniences. "And the children of 1912," she writes, "prefer comfort to poetry." Her new house she means to love as dearly as she did her old abode. Yet she knows that a faithful affection will often lead her back to her former home to revisit the rooms where she spent so many happy years.

Maternity came to Marcelle Tinayre early, when she was still in her teens. "I became a mother too young and without having wished it," she writes. As her novels show, she is not one of those women who adore babies. "Mere sketches, the spawn of humanity," she calls them. "Squirming, gurgling, red little objects." This is not the language of the baby-worshipper. How different it is from the maternal tenderness with which one of our own novelists, man though he be, Mr. W. J. Locke, describes the little foundling which Aristide Pujol on one of his Joyous Adventures picked up on the road. This wee scrap of humanity "goo'ed pleasantly, his tiny fingers clutched the man's hand and seemed to close round his heart," then "the clasp relaxed, puckers appeared at the corners of the dribbling mouth, and a myriad tiny horizontal lines of care marked the baby's brow."

No such sympathetic picture of babyhood appears in Madame Tinayre's novels. An insusceptibility to infantile charms is the one unfeminine feature of her disposition. Yet she makes up for her inappreciation of babyhood by a fondness for older children. She was not without maternal instinct, though it was long in awaking. How as her son and daughters grew out of infancy she came to love them with a passionate devotion, is revealed in *Madeleine au Miroir*, in the two chapters entitled "La Mère et le Fils" and "Les Enfants." In the latter, there is a passage recalling an earlier one in *La Maison du Péché*, where with keen insight Madame Tinayre analyses the psychology of a mother's love for her son, "one of the profoundest and most mysterious of sentiments . . . akin to the passion of love." "It has its secret origin," she writes, "in the pride and wonder of a woman who has created a being different from herself and who begins in him a life which is not a continuation of her own but a transposition. In our daughters, we recognize our own childhood and youth, just as after many years one re-reads a fine book which has been half forgotten. Our sons are a new book, surprising, disconcerting, pathetic, and difficult to decipher."

Yet even a daughter may display astonishing characteristics. In "Les Enfants" Madame Tinayre marvels at her little Annette's passion for dolls, a passion which her mother had never known. "At three years old, when she herself was but a living doll, Annette knew instinctively how to hold and handle her inert nurslings and with an adroitness which promised all the grace and dignity of motherhood."

On her establishment in Paris, Marcelle Tinayre found herself in one of the most literary and artistic circles of the metropolis. Her sister had married the late M. Pelletan, the well-known publisher and the intimate friend of Anatole France. Another member of the Tinayre circle was the brilliant essayist Marcel Schwob. He and his charming wife had gathered round them the choicest spirits of the capital in a literary salon, which was visited also by distinguished foreigners staying in Paris. Robert Louis Stevenson was frequently their guest and his friend Sir Sidney Colvin. By so cultured a company we may be sure that Madame Tinayre's striking literary gifts were quickly appreciated.

Those gifts she was already displaying in her novels. She was barely nineteen when her first published work, *Avant l'Amour*, appeared in *La Nouvelle Revue*. Before accepting it, the editress, Madame Juliette Adam, sent the manuscript, signed with a masculine pseudonym, to Alphonse Daudet. On returning it, Daudet wrote, "The story displays inexperience, but you must publish it; for this young man will be some one."

In 1897, la Société du Mercure de France published the novel in volume form. Then in quick succession followed *La Rançon*, *Hellé*, and *L'Oiseau d'Orage*. In 1902, in *La Maison du Péché*, Madame Tinayre attained to what has so far been the high-water mark of her genius. In *La Vie Amoureuse de François Barbazanges* she produced a work of great excellence, inspired by her study of the seventeenth century, and in its subtle whimsical phantasy standing apart from all her other novels. The seven volumes which followed at fairly regular intervals from 1905 down to the present year are all more characteristic of her genius.

Unlike most of her fellow countrywomen Madame Tinayre is a traveller. The mysteries of the custom-house, of railway timetables, and of foreign languages have no terrors for her. She is not one of those Frenchwomen who go about encumbered with a dozen trunks. She can pack in ten minutes, and without hesitation pronounce the few necessary words in almost any European tongue. Why should not Frenchwomen travel and travel alone ? she asks. Why, whenever they are seen abroad unaccompanied, are they always supposed to be courting certain danger or engaging in a secret intrigue ? When put to it they are just as capable as their English sisters of looking after themselves.

Madame Tinayre has visited England

several times and has taken one journey, if not more, to the Near East, where she had relatives in Adrianople. During their residence in Paris she had made friends with several leaders of the Young Turk Revolution. And it was partly to visit her friends, the Young Turks, that in the spring of the eventful year 1909 our author started for Constantinople. On the way she heard of the counter-revolution of April 13. The nearest French Consul advised her to go home. "You will see nothing at Constantinople," he said. "All the shops and banks are closed. The streets are full of soldiers crying 'Long live the Sultan and the Law of Cheriat.' These are the soldiers who, on April 13, killed three hundred officers, a few deputies or ministers, and a crowd of loafers. The boats are full of tourists who are returning. All you could do in Constantinople would be to stay shut up in your hotel. You would see nothing. What is the use of going ?"

But with what she describes as invincible feminine obstinacy, Madame Tinayre persisted. "I can assure you," she replied to the Consul, "I shall not stay shut up in my hotel. At the worst, I shall look out of my window at the passers-by and I shall hear them talking. If there is a disturbance, I may be a little afraid, not much, and afterwards I shall be glad for once to have tasted fire."

The Consul laughed, and his undaunted countrywoman continued her journey. She reached Constantinople ; and there she heard and saw a great deal. Among other stirring events she witnessed the arrival of the Macedonian troops in the capital, the return of the Young Turks to power, and the deposition of Abdul Hamid. All this and much more she has related in her book, *Notes d'une Voyageuse en Turquie*, to which recent events lend a special interest.

One of the most prominent figures in the Young Turk movement, Ahmed-Riza Bey, President of the Ottoman Chamber, Madame Tinayre had known in Paris, when he was living in modest rooms in the Square Monge, editing his paper, *The Mechveret*,[1] and attending Positivist meetings. In this philosophic circle he excited ardent sympathy because

[1] A revolutionary newspaper in Turkish and Arabic, devoted to advocating the overthrow of Abdul Hamid.

of his unhappy exile, his apparent honesty, his grand air, and his proud poverty. He was proud indeed, very proud and extremely self-reliant. Once, having fallen seriously ill, he nearly died rather than communicate with his friends. And it was only by chance that an English sympathiser, discovering his plight, was able to render the service necessary for his recovery.

"He looked," writes Madame Tinayre, "like some philosopher Caliph or young King of the Magi. . . . And it seemed so charming that he should be a Turk, a real Turk. I remember meeting him in a studio, at a fancy-dress ball. Many Turks were there, but they were pseudo-Turks. He, Ahmed-Riza, in Western dress clothes, looked like the only Parisian present, until, with imperturbable seriousness, he admitted that the dancing, the low necks and the fancy costumes disgusted him. Then we understood that he was not a Parisian at all, but a true Turk in heart and soul."

Still more forcibly was her friend's nationality borne in upon Madame Tinayre when after the return of the Young Turks to power she saw him at home, at Constantinople, in the haremlik of his brother-in-law's house, surrounded by his female relatives. Ahmed-Riza's sister, Selma, a well-known figure among advanced Turkish women, had disguised her French friend as a Turkish lady. Clothed in a tcharchaf of black silk, hooded and veiled, accompanied by a slave and a Turkish woman friend, the travestied traveller made her entrance into the brilliantly lighted, luxuriously furnished salon of the haremlik. Near his mother, an aged, wrinkled lady reclining on a divan, stood Ahmed-Riza Bey. He welcomed the visitors with cold dignity, never dreaming of advancing to meet them or of shaking hands as he would have done at Paris. "He has become Turk again," thought his French friend, "and he has assumed the reserved, indifferent attitude of his countrymen. He does not even raise his eyes. Doubtless this indiscreet visit annoys him. And I flatter myself that he is disappointed. For a moment through my thick tulle veil I observe him, comparing him to the Ahmed-Riza I used to know. . . . He is just as grave as of yore, but more majestic, very much President of the Chamber. . . . Then, one of his sisters, going behind me, raises my veil. . . . Ahmed-Riza recognizes me. His face lights up with amused surprise. He holds out his hand and exclaims . . ."

"He is not at all shocked. He even says he is charmed to see me in the garb he loves, that severe, mysterious, not unbecoming costume, which, now that I have worn it of my own free will, I shall forbear to criticize on my return to France. And I promise never to speak ill of it."

That in Ahmed-Riza Bey which most interested Madame Tinayre was his concern for the education of his countrywomen. His residence in the West had shown him that women are worth educating. One of the first uses he had made of his new power had been to obtain from Abdul Hamid a magnificent palace in which he had established a school for girls.[1] But unfortunately his aims were misrepresented; he was considered to have some private axe to grind, and this very undertaking was ultimately to lead to his fall.

Some of the most interesting pages of *Les*

[1] See article in *Daily Chronicle*, November 2, 1911, entitled "Emancipation of Moslem girls, Ahmed-Riza Bey's Great Scheme."

Notes d'une Voyageuse are devoted to a study of Turkish women. Madame Tinayre describes all classes and all grades of intelligence from the doll-like wives of Abdul Hamid to the highly cultured sisters of Ahmed-Riza and their friends. Repeating what was told her by the station officials and the officers of the royal escort, she relates how by night the eleven ladies whom the deposed Sultan was permitted to carry into captivity were brought with their lord and master to the railway station of Sirkedji.

"In the cold greyness which precedes dawn, a few servants and eunuchs helped the eleven women out of their carriages. . . . The ladies, veiled in white yachmaks, were wrapped in evening cloaks of silk and lace, not very suitable travelling attire, but Burberrys and fur coats are not included in a sultana's trousseau. . . . Very paternally Abdul Hamid showed his wives and his son into a carriage of the special train. And then he asked for lemonade, which the station refreshment-room could not produce.

"While the engine was getting up steam, the ladies in the lace cloaks amused themselves by examining the railway carriage which had been transformed into a haremlik. Natives of wild Circassia, they had been bought quite young. And all they knew of the world was the closed gardens of the palace, with their marble kiosks filled with treasures, their menageries, their aviaries, and the boats on the lake. A few, it appears, well guarded, used to cycle and motor through the gardens. But not one of them had ever crossed to Stamboul. Not one had the vaguest idea of a station, of a railway carriage, or of that strange beast, a locomotive engine.

"Now the wonders of civilization suddenly burst upon them. They tried the arm-chairs of the Pullman car, they played with the blue blinds, they chattered, smoked, laughed, and even forgot to veil their faces. But the fallen despot was indulgent. He cared for their comfort and continued to ask for the lemonade which was not forthcoming."

With equally vivid touch Madame Tinayre describes the emancipated women whom she met in Constantinople. Of a type unknown in Western Europe was the intelligent but uncivilized revolutionary, the Lady of Salonica, with a face as wrinkled as a winter apple, and iron-grey hair flatly braided.

She wore a plain grey skirt, and in Paris might have been mistaken for a washer-woman. But she had carried revolvers hidden in biscuit-tins, and letters concealed in the pockets of her tcharchaf. She penetrated everywhere and watched everything. Had the Young Turks paid heed to her warnings they might never have been driven from power.

The Lady of Salonica's friend, Mélek Hanoum, is a *désenchantée,* who is quite proud of her unhappy domestic experiences. She considers herself highly civilized ; and those magic words " progress," " civilization," are for ever on her lips. She talks of Kant as if he were some good old uncle. She calls herself a deist. She boasts of having studied French philosophy in the works of Voltaire, Lamartine, and Zola. And when Madame Tinayre smiles at the last name, she cries, " What ! you are laughing. . . . Don't you think Zola is a great philosopher ? I didn't like him at first, because he writes too plainly about nature. But later, when I understood progress and civilization, I loved Zola. Yes, he is a great philosopher, but I don't like the way he writes of love."

Mélek Hanoum is too patriotic and too modern not to be a revolutionary and a member of the Committee of Union and Progress. Yet she has not discarded her femininity. She still adores jewels and pretty frocks and powder. She is a Turk to the marrow of her bones, and yet she worships everything French. She is horrified to find that in Paris for two years women have ceased to wear skirts with foundations, while she is still wearing one. "Yes, I am wearing one, and with frills too," she cries scandalised. "Oh, I will have it removed at once." She nearly dies with laughing when Madame Tinayre tells her that advanced feminists in Paris cut their hair short and wear coats of masculine cut.

Of a very different type from her friend, Mélek Hanoum, is the tall, stately Selma Hanoum, sister of Ahmed-Riza Bey. Mélek is a dreamer ; Selma is actual, courageous, and plentifully endowed with common sense. If nature had made her a man she would have played an important part in her country's history. Madame Tinayre had known her in Paris, where she had joined her brother. Now she tells of her brother's flight during the counter-revolution and of her own escape in disguise from a reactionary mob. "Even to-day," she adds, "it would be unsafe for me to go into the quarter of the fanatics, so bitterly have they slandered me. . . . And why?" she asks sadly. "I have never incited my sisters to be imprudent. I never believed that any real reform of manners could be achieved in a few months. Was it a crime to dream of some better system of feminine education, of something more effectual in the way of legal protection for women and of obtaining for them that minimum of liberty which is indispensable for the development and dignity of every human being?"

We have dwelt at considerable length on this book of Turkish travel not only because of the special interest it possesses in the light of present happenings, but because in the passages on Turkish women it is very typical of the author's manner. Every character lives as a vivid portrait, the doll-like little sultanas playing with the blue blinds of their railway carriage, the equally feminine Mélek Hanoum only with her Oriental femininity thinly veiled by a veneer of Western learning, and the two downright revolutionaries, the uncivilized spy and the statesman-like Selma.

This feminine portion of *Les Notes d'une Voyageuse* is thus the prototype of all Madame Tinayre's work, the great merit of which consists in its presentation of a striking gallery of feminine portraits, each with a strong individuality, a marked idiosyncrasy of her own. Madame Tinayre is essentially a woman's novelist. Her heart is open to all women. No woman is my enemy she has said even during the War. Every kind of femininity save one she has depicted, but there is one type of woman who is conspicuous by absence from her gallery : the new woman of to-day as she appears in this country and in America, the bachelor woman who has herself so well in hand that she seems totally unsexed, *le Neutre* as Anatole France calls her. Perhaps Madame Tinayre has never met *un neutre,* or perhaps for her they do not exist. For we can well imagine that her keen eye may pierce beneath the mask of indifference and coldness to the femininity which is hidden away from every other observer. "And you yourself, Miss ——," says Madame Tinayre, addressing the most modern of all bachelor women, "I did not for one moment doubt your sex, for you are a pretty girl, fresh and fair. . . . I liked your droll little nose and your intelligent eyes, looking fearlessly at persons, things, and ideas."

Madame Tinayre herself is far from being a new woman. She is too deeply engrossed in primitive things—in love, in marriage, and in maternity. On some of these subjects she holds quite old-fashioned ideas. Above all things a woman should be womanly she thinks, and on that ground she condemns the militant suffrage movement. The women of to-day have in her opinion lost much of the grace and the charm of the last generation. The lot of the modern bachelor woman she holds to be less happy than the life of an old maid in the past. The latter may have kept parrots and been a trifle ridiculous, yet she brought up her nephews and nieces, she received the new-born infant into her arms, she scolded the naughty schoolboy, she taught the little girls knitting, and she kept her heart warm by this pseudo-maternity, whereas the empty heart of the single woman of to-day, compelled to compete with men for a livelihood, withers and shrivels away in loneliness. "The woman of to-day misses everything when she misses love."

Such opinions are perhaps somewhat surprising in one who in other respects is so modern as Madame Tinayre. Yet we shall be less astonished when we remember how large a part family life plays in France. If our author knew more of England, if she saw what happy, crowded and eventful lives English spinsters lead, she might possibly modify her view. In all other respects, we repeat, Madame Tinayre is essentially modern. She is eagerly anxious for the removal of restraints, economic, social, and religious, which impede the progress of her sex.

Her feminine ideal, she has written, is a creature with the body of a woman, the heart of a man, and the head of an angel.

The theme of all her novels is love represented by the eternal duel between the sexes. This duel she describes as it is fought by all classes, all types and almost all ages of women, from the young girl in her first novel, *Avant l'Amour*, down to the middle-aged woman, Madeleine Mirande, in *Madeleine au Miroir*.

And what of the other party in this duel, what of men? Madame Tinayre writes from the woman's standpoint, and on the whole men play a secondary part in her novels. There is one striking exception, however, *La Maison du Péché;* Augustin de Chanteprie not Fanny Manolé is the protagonist of this novel. Yet Augustin, the ascetic, the recluse, is in reality more feminine than the more robust heroine, Fanny, who is a woman of the world. In point of masculinity Madame Tinayre's strongest characters are the two doctors, Chaumette in *L'Oiseau d'Orage*, and Cayrol in *L'Ombre de l'Amour*.

Love, the grand *motif* of Madame Tinayre's work, she always considers apart from marriage. It is unnecessary to say that this is the essentially French point of view. In a recent work, *Prejugé et Problème des Sexes*, by that distinguished writer, Jean Finot, occurs this sentence: "Have not the courts of love themselves decreed that love and marriage are as hostile to one another as fire and water?"[1] If such was the finding of mediæval courts of love, the same conditions

[1] Les cours de l'amour n'ont elle pas decrété que l'amour et le marriage s'excluent comme l'eau et le feu?

too often exist to-day in a country where marriages are generally made for convenience. In the opinion of Madame Tinayre and of many other French writers the young girl married out of the school-room to a husband much older than herself, with whom she is probably but slightly acquainted, will most likely fall in love with a man who is not her husband. Whether she succumbs to the passion depends on her temperament and training. The husband, for his part, is likely to grow tired of a girl wife, who has had no experience of the world, and he will probably seek distraction outside his home. These are the incidents which occupy French novelists, who plead in their justification that matrimonial love, though it does certainly exist in French life, is neglected in French literature, simply because it has no story.

Even when her characters are free to marry, as, for example, Augustin de Chanteprie and Fanny Manolé in *La Maison du Péché*, and Josanne and Noël in *La Rebelle*, the question of their legal union is for Madame Tinayre a secondary matter. Her point of view is that of a heroine of Anatole France, Thérèse in *Le Lys Rouge*, whom Miss Bell asks for advice as to her marriage with an Italian Prince. "'You are not a child,'" Thérèse replies. "'If you love and are loved, do what you think right and don't complicate love by material interests which have nothing to do with feeling. That is the true advice of a friend!'

"For a moment Miss Bell failed to understand. Then she blushed and rose. She was shocked."

And like Miss Bell, many English readers will be shocked by Madame Tinayre's novels, except perhaps one, *Hellé*, and her last book, *Madeleine au Miroir*. *Hellé* is a novel which may be safely left on the drawing-room table or put into the hand of "the young person." But no one should form an opinion of Madame Tinayre's novels therefrom. In power and insight, in character drawing and in artistic composition, *Hellé* ranks far below our author's other works. She herself has said, "If you wish to read one of my novels, don't choose *Hellé, c'est ennuyeux*."

As, after this warning, no one will read *Hellé*, we may briefly summarize the story: a young orphan girl, born and bred in the provinces, in early maidenhood is brought to Paris by an elderly uncle. There two suitors present themselves: one is a young poet, handsome, brilliantly clever, but superficial and, as it appears later, disloyal; the other, a much older man, is also a man of letters and clever too, but in a different way from his rival, with less sparkle, more weight, and fewer physical attractions. At the time of the uncle's death, the brilliant admirer, Maurice, is abroad; and it is to the care of his graver rival, Antoine, that the dying man commits his niece. "Hellé shall be my sister," says Antoine. But he hopes that she may become something more. And his hopes seem likely to be realized until Maurice returns from the Near East. He comes bringing with him a dramatic poem which is to take the world by storm, and announces that he has had thrilling adventures. Hellé falls a victim to his fascination. She becomes engaged to him. Then gradually, but fortunately before the marriage, she begins to discover his faults and to find him a mere braggart who basely betrays his friends. His Eastern adventures turn out to have been nothing at all. There is no meanness to which he will not descend in order to further his worldly advancement. The engagement is broken off. The faithful Antoine is still waiting, and ultimately he receives his reward.

It is a pretty story, but not, as we have said, typical of Madame Tinayre's work. In her other novels she has been accused by an English critic of dealing too frankly with the passion of love. But a French critic has written of her: "I do not think that there is any novelist among our contemporaries who knows so well how to study, how to handle, how to take apart and put together love in itself."

This subtle analysis of love, in the phase of its awakening in a young girl's heart, is the theme of Madame Tinayre's first novel, *Avant l'Amour*. Every one who is interested in Madame Tinayre's talent should read this book, for it contains the germ of all her subsequent work. Yet, though she was very young when she wrote it, this novel is by no means milk for babes; it is strong meat. Here, with marvellous inspiration, this young writer penetrated into the mysteries of love. With wonderful intuition she wrote things, of which in those days, as she has herself since confessed, she did not then completely grasp the whole import. The novel contains crudities resulting, as Alphonse Daudet said, from inexperience; but it also contains passages of power and insight which the author has never surpassed.

In Madame Tinayre's second novel, *La Rançon*, as in *Hellé*, which was to follow it, we have two types of men, one young, gay, thoughtless and brilliant; the other older, graver and more serious. But in *La Rançon* the woman, Jacqueline, is no longer free to choose between them. Marriage bonds and a son unite her to the thoughtless and superficial Paul, although as time goes on she becomes painfully aware that her heart belongs to his serious friend, Etienne. The conflict between love and duty is the theme of this book. At first love conquers, and Jacqueline becomes the mistress of her husband's friend.

For a while the lovers are rapturously happy. Etienne forgets his disloyalty to Paul. Jacqueline finds in her lover a kindred soul capable of satisfying all her aspirations in a measure which her husband had never been able to do. But gradually the moulding influence of this great passion converts her from a gay butterfly into a serious, thoughtful woman. Her husband's claims upon her fidelity are brought home to her by his serious illness. Her conscience awakes. And it is her conscience which finally parts her from her lover. In his farewell letter of renunciation Etienne writes: "Jacqueline, Jacqueline, one obstacle separates us, more formidable than any law, your conscience. . . . By a sacrifice, which is almost beyond human strength, I am paying the ransom of our superhuman happiness."

In *La Rançon* Madame Tinayre was feeling her way; she was still serving her apprenticeship, she had not yet fulfilled the promise of her first novel, *Avant l'Amour*. That remained for her next book, *La Maison du Péché*. Here we still have the conflict between love and duty, but treated in a more masterly manner, lifted to a higher plane, than in *La Rançon*, and with religion intervening.

In *La Maison du Péché* it is not the marriage bond that opposes love, but filial devotion and loyalty to ancestral faith. Moreover, the conflict of these two opposing forces is intensified by the conflict between two temperaments, the paganism of the heroine, Fanny Manolé, and the religious asceticism of the hero, Augustin de Chanteprie. Etienne in *La Rançon* is able to appreciate and even admire Jacqueline's conscience, which has evolved under his influence. The pagan mind of Fanny and the Christian conscience of Augustin are eternally hostile. "They were not of the same race. They did not speak the same language. Love, uniting them for a moment, left them more sorrowful than before, with a vague feeling of shame and of deception."

Such a conflict was bound to end in tragedy. It could not culminate in the rational renunciation with which *La Rançon* closes.

The scene of *La Maison du Péché* is laid in the country, in a little town not far from Paris and yet so provincial that it might be hundreds of miles away. In an old-fashioned mansion, cut off from the world by high garden walls and dense linden groves, live Augustin de Chanteprie, a youth who has never been young, and his saintly mother. Their life is that of a convent. Their ancestors were Jansenists ; and with all the Puritanical rigour and asceticism of their forbears Madame de Chanteprie and her son practise the Catholic faith.

Yet in the windows of every soul, however closely shuttered against worldly glamour, there is ever some tiny chink through which may penetrate now and again a reminder of material things. Such a reminder, only a few paces from their own door, was ever present to Madame de Chanteprie and Augustin in a garden house, known as "La Maison du Péché," built and adorned in classical style by a backsliding Voltairean ancestor for an actress, who was his mistress.

Little dreaming that one day the old story would repeat itself in her son's life, Madame de Chanteprie, on the day after Augustin's first Communion, banished him to the house in the garden, there to pursue his studies under the direction of the austere Abbé Forgerus. And there, in a room, which his pagan ancestor had decorated with garlands of poppies and pictures of heathen goddesses, Augustin, until his twentieth year, lived the life of a recluse.

Only once a day did the devout Abbé permit him to visit his sainted mother. He endeavoured to break off the boy's friendly intercourse with his old nurse, Jacqueline, whose knowledge of the healing properties of herbs suggested dealings with the Evil One. For the Abbé Forgerus woman was the enemy ; and he taught his pupil to regard her as a corrupt creature to be feared and avoided ; for the saint who sins seven times a day, he said, sins six times because of a woman.

But, with the exception of his mother, whom he venerated as a Saint Monica, of her friend, an aged spinster, who was as simple as a child, and of the old peasant woman their servant, no woman ever crossed Augustin's path until he was nineteen.

Then it was that the young recluse first realized the attractions of femininity. With subtle insight and minute detail Madame Tinayre describes this awakening. It happened one summer day. Augustin was walking in the garden, when his eye was attracted by a woman's red hair caught among the bushes. It belonged to a humble maiden, the old servant's niece, employed to pick fruit in the garden. Augustin watched her over the hedge, observing the childlike contour of her face, the fairness of her neck, and her arms and hands stained with the red juice of the currants she was picking. If the girl had looked round and seen him watching her he would have died with shame. Then suddenly he turned and fled. Shutting himself into the darkened room of the garden house, he realized that something terrible and never to be forgotten had entered into his life, that this bewilderment of soul, this fever in the blood must be that of which he had read in his holy books. And on his knees before the crucifix, Augustin beat his breast, repenting of his guilty curiosity.

This awakening of the senses was but the prelude to an experience much more fundamental and lasting in its consequences.

A lady from Paris purchases a farm-house on the Chanteprie estate and settles there her adopted niece, Fanny Manolé, a fascinating young widow of six-and-twenty. Augustin and Fanny become interested in one another. And as the young man's interest grows he becomes possessed by curiosity as to the religious position of his new acquaintance. Being too shy to inquire, he brings the village priest to Fanny's cottage. And there, during the course of conversation, it transpires that

Madame Manolé is a pure pagan. As they come away from the cottage, the village priest counsels his young friend either to flee from Fanny or to convert her. And when Augustin asks why, the priest tells him he is in love. Although Augustin denies this at first, on looking into his own heart, he is constrained to admit that the priest had said true; yet he tells himself that what he loves in Fanny is not her beauty but her soul.

"Fanny was not the feminine animal against which M. Forgerus had warned him. Neither was she the seductress or the wife. She was simply a soul."

Here the author is developing the same theme she had treated in her teens. Augustin, like the missionary of Patmos, resolves to save this soul. And Fanny, who loves her serious suitor, is quite ready to be saved. "Persuade me, convince me," she says; "I will do all you wish, I will believe everything."

But Fanny did not know her own rebellious heart. In that moment of rapture she could not foresee that none of the arguments of the priest, whom Augustin charged with her instruction, that not even her love for Augustin himself, could make a mystic of her rational soul or resolve the doubts of her unbelieving mind.

Fanny was too sincere to feign conversion. Even Augustin had begun to realize that what he loved in Fanny was something more than her soul. Then she, writes Madame Tinayre, "shaking the dust from her feet on the threshold of the temple, wherein she had found nought but words and phantoms . . . like the vintager to the vineyard, went forth towards love. . . . And gently, shyly, repeating in an inverse sense the methods that Augustin had adopted towards her, she dreamed of conquering the one who had failed to conquer, of converting this ardent Christian to the only religion of life." Fanny succeeded where Augustin had failed. But Madame de Chanteprie imposes as a condition of her consent to their marriage that Fanny shall become a Catholic. During the mother's temporary absence from home, the old scenes are re-enacted in the garden house. And there comes a moment when, in answer to Fanny's triumphant question, "Do you love me?" Augustin cries: "I love you." "More than your salvation? Even to sin?" persists his mistress. "Even to damnation and to eternal death," he answers.

But to such a temperament remorse was inevitable. After a prolonged conflict of soul Augustin leaves Fanny. "She was lost, lost, his beloved! Neither his affection nor his sacrifice could help her. Why had he not been worthy to save her soul?" "Let God's will be done, not mine," he murmured. Yet, though the words of resignation were on his lips, doubt and despair clouded his heart.

Augustin had made the supreme sacrifice; but he had lost all interest in life; and life ebbed from him.

Even his faith had vanished. Darkness thickened around him. "Night is falling," he cried, and, with these words on his lips, he passed into the great unknown.

This book, like the *Thaïs* of M. Anatole France, with which it constantly challenges comparison, is a very powerful indictment of the ascetic ideal.

Sacrifice, one rational and resigned, the other sore and bleeding as the heart's deep wound, had been the theme of Madame Tinayre's two novels, *La Rançon* and *La*

Maison du Péché. In another powerful story, *La Rebelle*, she depicts not self-sacrifice but self-realization. Josanne Valentin, passing through bitter sorrows and a terrible deception, succeeds at length in living down slander, in overcoming prejudice and in dispelling the mistrust of the man who loves her and whom she loves. She escapes from those terrible *convenances et conventions* of which women are the eternal victims; she succeeds in attaining our author's feminine ideal of a creature possessing an angel's head, a man's heart, and a woman's body.

La Rebelle is the most frank of all Madame Tinayre's books. No one who would know her views as to woman's destiny should neglect to read it and to mark the following significant paragraph:

"I think," says Josanne, "of all the women I am about to see, whom I shall question as to their life, their character, their tastes—I think of the women doctors, barristers, professors, artists, whose successes are related in the *Monde Féminin*. They are the feminine élite, the emancipated, the rebels. . . . They revolt against prejudice and conventional morality. They are recreating a new ideal of honour, virtue, and feminine duty. Their minds are clear, their hearts noble. . . . And yet, no sooner do we begin to talk freely, as woman to woman, than I guess the secret of their inner life, I feel that they have retained all the old feminine instincts of the past. . . . Man may find them in his way, competing with him in schools, in hospitals, in business ; but in the home and the family the old order persists. . . . With her whole heart and with all her senses woman aspires to the servitude of love. . . . She has not the courage of her liberty. . . . Her one desire and her one regret is love. Let her lover trample upon her, she will kiss his feet and say : 'Do it again !' "

This passage is in itself enough to prove that Madame Tinayre is no feminist as we in England to-day understand the term. Though every woman will protest that here Madame Tinayre exaggerates, no woman will deny that her words contain a germ of profound truth. Yet we venture to think that in a woman's love maternal pity is a more powerful factor than any mean desire for servitude. That this may be the case Madame Tinayre admits in a later novel.

That pity is the inspiration of love, and even, in a measure, its substitute, is the theme of Madame Tinayre's powerful book, *L'Ombre de l'Amour*. How far love and how far pity enter into the sentiment which leads the country doctor's daughter, Denise Cayrol, to give herself to her father's consumptive patient, is difficult to know, and one doubts whether Denise herself knew. On the other hand it is quite clear that pity alone inspires the little seamstress, Fortunade, to care for the wounded poacher, Veydrenne, and to visit this brutal brigand in his lair. The kindness of both these women leads to their ruin.

The story of Fortunade, secretly stealing by night to the poacher's den, is vividly told. Veydrenne was noted throughout the country-side for his unscrupulous brutality. Only that afternoon he had set his dogs upon the doctor who had called to see him. But it was this very deed which stirred Fortunade's heart and made her resolve to go and tend the wounded man.

Before setting out for the lonely hut in

which Veydrenne and his father were living, Fortunade enters the church and kneels before the altar. Her mind is full of conflicting thoughts—she knows that men will condemn what she is about to do; she has already committed sin in lying to her parents as to the cause of her evening absence. Yet she believes that charity comes before everything, and that the salvation of a sufferer may often atone for a falsehood.

Ignorant of theological subtlety, her simple soul rebels against the mystery of pain. . . . How could it be reconciled with God's goodness? How could the sight of suffering fail to kindle holy wrath? Kind people, like Dr. Cayrol and the priest, for example, who saw human misery in all its horror and who tried to relieve it, did not seem to let it disturb their equanimity. . . . They tended the dying, they listened to the cries of mothers and widows—and, with their emotion swiftly lulled by custom, accepting with resignation their powerlessness in the face of social or natural calamity, they returned to their homes. . . . They forgot. Fortunade did not forget. . . . Christian pity filled her heart at the story of Christ's suffering, not that whining, cowardly pity which lulls itself with tears and phrases and mysticity. Her pity took the form of a resolve immediately expressed in action. In that Limousin maiden with the sad eyes and feeble body there lived again the soul of the virgins who overthrew idols and braved proconsuls, the soul of those heroic shepherdesses who, obeying heavenly voices, cast aside the distaff and seized the sword. But it was not to any grand mission or glorious martyrdom, so Fortunade thought, that her voices summoned her, they merely called her to repair the injustice created by the vicissitudes of nature and the egoism of men. . . . They bade her (in obedience to the command of the Crucified, who admitted into Paradise the good thief—and perhaps the bad one too) feed the hungry, clothe the naked, comfort those who weep, stir the feelings of those who have forgotten how to weep, give light to those in darkness, speech to the dumb, strength to the broken, guidance to the lost. . . . What a wonderful temptation! What holy madness! What magnificent hope! . . . How to resist it! She must think! But why? God Himself is speaking. To the consoler he is revealing her vocation. " Go ! hasten to your brother, who suffers ! Not to-morrow, but to-night ! " She shudders. " But if people knew ! What would they say ? Did not Monsieur Cayrol call me mad and accuse me of being in love ? But you, Virgin Mary, you can read my heart."

And Fortunade went. Alone in the darkness she sped over moor and fen to the poacher's lonely hut. And, like another Pitying One, while saving others herself she could not save. But of the little peasant's soul may not that be true which the four evangelists have said of a man's life that whosoever, for the sake of that Pitying One, shall lose his life shall find it ?

It is not Christian pity which inspires Fortunade's mistress, Denise. She is a pagan. Her religion is the religion of humanity. But the penalty of the sacrifice of herself to Jean Favière, her father's consumptive patient, Denise alone is not able to pay. " Man is a coward in the face of death, woman is a coward in the face of suffering. Pity becomes the accomplice of egoism. . . . And suffering creatures are born." Thus the sacrifice of Denise raises the problem which her own father discusses in the third chapter of the book. Dr. Cayrol, little dreaming of the misfortune that was to fall upon his daughter, does not hesitate to condemn as abominable any union between a healthy and a diseased person. In the words of the doctor who attends Denise at her confinement, "Tuberculosis is not hereditary." Yet the child of Jean Favière, the consumptive, runs a great risk of becoming consumptive in his turn. His children too will be especially susceptible to infection and will poison the race.

Such is the theme of this powerful book. In the hands of a writer less artistic than Madame Tinayre, the story might have been morbid. Here and in *La Rebelle* she has written something like a problem novel. If one considered these two books alone one might rank her with those new writers who belong to what is termed *l'école de la vie.* Yet not even in these two novels does Madame Tinayre's innate feeling for form ever forsake her. Never has she described country life with greater insight and more artistic power than in *L'Ombre de l'Amour.* Pervading the whole book is the romantic atmosphere of the superstitious, legend-loving Limousin of her birth, with all its wild savagery only hidden by the thinnest veneer of civilization, its wolves and poachers and brigands, living vividly in these pages. Some of her finest descriptive passages are to be found in her picture of the midnight mass in the village church and of the previous assembling of the worshippers in the village tavern. No reader of this book will be surprised to learn that it is the author's work of predilection.

Two of the best of Madame Tinayre's shorter stories are *L'Oiseau d'Orage* and *La Consolatrice*. The former Edouard Rod described as "one of the most perfect and delightful stories that I know." It is the tale of a happy wife seduced by an unscrupulous, egotistical gallant, whom the kind but simple-hearted husband introduces into the home. Denarcys, the betrayer, is as brutal and selfish a creature as Robert Greslou in Bourget's *Disciple*. He entraps the wife, Marthe Chaumette, who never, even after her fall, forfeits our respect. As soon as he hears that his mistress is to bear a child, the lover abandons her, leaving Marthe in an agony of doubt as to whether her infant is the child of her husband or of her lover. Marthe drinks the cup of suffering to the dregs. Yet the story ends happily. And we leave Marthe, having paid to the full the penalty of her fault, winning her way back to a serene and faithful existence.

La Consolatrice is perhaps the most striking of all Madame Tinayre's shorter stories, and in the power of its psychological analysis the most subtle and the most profound. George Clarence, the musician, married to a commonplace *bourgeoise*, is the lover of a great *prima donna*. She perishes in a theatre fire. The wife, who is aware of the relations between her husband and the dead woman, herself announces to Clarence the terrible tidings of the calamity. Confronted with the sorrow of the husband, whom in her matter-of-fact way she loves, Madame Clarence develops into a noble, tender-hearted woman. Patiently and tactfully she rescues the musician from the verge of madness, winning him back to comparative peace of mind.

In *Madeleine au Miroir*, one of Madame Tinayre's most recent and most artistic books, she has given us a fascinating study of middle-aged femininity. Certain novels, that morbid book, *L'Age Dangereux,* for example, represent the woman who is approaching the meridian of life as necessarily erratic if not a little insane. Madeleine, on the contrary, never loses her balance. If, during the year of Agadir her mother's heart wished for a moment that if war must come it will come speedily, before her son is of an age to fight, she quickly chides herself for the selfishness of such a thought. Gazing into the past, looking forward with some trepidation to the future, and much concerned with the present, Madeleine at her mirror weaves a delicate tissue of brilliant social sketches, of patriotic rural landscapes and delicate autobiographical recollections, interspersed with reflections on morals, manners, and current events, and traversed by a romantic plot.

Madeleine is perhaps the most autobiographical of Marcelle Tinayre's books. Yet it is impossible to think of her as middle-aged. Her sparkling eyes, her slender form, her winning manner are still those of youth. In this book, like so many of her countrywomen, she anticipates her years, she betrays a somewhat premature desire to accept gracefully middle age. For her, life moves swiftly, revealing new duties, new responsibilities, new joys, and new sorrows. Yet she never penned truer words than when she wrote: "The spring of love and life sings within me as in the morning of my youth."

ROMAIN ROLLAND

THE WORKS OF ROMAIN ROLLAND

1895. Les Origines du théatre lyrique moderne. Histoire de l'opéra en Europe avant Lulli et Scarlatti.

1898. Les Loups. (Play.)

1899. Le Triomphe de la Raison. (Play.)

1901. Danton. (Play.)

1902. Le 14 Juillet. (Play.)

1903. Le Temps Viendra. (Play.)
Le Théatre du Peuple.
Beethoven. (Les Maîtres de la Musique.)

1904. La Montespan. (Play.)

1905. Jean Christophe : L'Aube.
Le Matin.
L'Adolescent.
Michel Ange. (Librairie de l'Art ancien et moderne.)

1906. Jean Christophe : La Révolte.

1907. Jean Christophe : La Foire sur la Place.

1907. Vie de Michel Ange. (Vies des Hommes Illustres.)
Vie de Beethoven. (Vies des Hommes Illustres.)

1908. Jean Christophe : Antoinette.
Musiciens d'Aujourd'hui.
Musiciens d'Autrefois.

1909. Jean Christophe : Dans la Maison.
Le Théatre de la Révolution (including "Le 14 Juillet," "Danton," "Les Loups," plays previously published separately).

1910. Haendel. (Les Maîtres de la Musique.)
Jean Christophe Les Amies.

1911. Vie de Tolstoi. (Vies des Hommes Illustres.)

1912. Jean Christophe : Le Buisson Ardent.

1913. Jean Christophe : La Nouvelle Journée.

ROMAIN ROLLAND, 1866

ONE of the most puzzling enigmas of present-day literary France is the personality of M. Romain Rolland. Here is a Frenchman born in the heart of France, of French descent, and yet with a temperament curiously un-French. Something that is Celtic, a great deal that is Teutonic,[1] one may trace in the mentality of this great writer; but of the influence of that Latin or romance element which as a rule dominates French culture, there is singularly little trace either in the man or in his work.

Here is an excellent example for those philosophers who maintain that racial influence is a mere myth. But let them beware of forming too hasty a conclusion. Ethnologists may yet claim M. Rolland for

[1] In the light of the terrible events Europe has been witnessing for the last six months the imputation of Teutonism sounds so like an accusation that it almost becomes necessary to assert the obvious fact that affinity with Goethe's race need not involve any taint of that brutality by which the modern German is defiling himself in the present War.

their own. For, after a careful study of his family history and of that part of France where he was born it will appear that his Teutonism is after all not so completely inexplicable.

A Teutonic strain ethnologists expect to find in the inhabitants of eastern France, which is next door to Germany. But M. Rolland comes from the Morvan, a hilly plateau in the middle of France. How came so central a region to produce any one so German? Let history explain. At present le Morvan is completely surrounded by French lands. It was not always so. A time there was when le Morvan lay upon the verge of the old kingdom of France, when it abutted on or was sometimes included within the great duchy of Burgundy. Now, for centuries, Burgundy, when not an independent duchy, was a border province adjacent to Germany and to Switzerland, inhabited by a race who, like M. Rolland's hero, Jean Christophe, blended harmoniously the salient features of Teutonic and Celtic culture.

Occupying outposts of the Celtic world and near neighbours to the Teutonic, Burgundians and Morvanais were themselves of Teutonic descent. Originally they were woodcutters in German forests. Then came a time when, driven westward by the exhaustion of their home timber, these German woodsmen settled on the richly wooded banks of the River Yonne. Here, at the junction of the Yonne and one of its tributaries, their descendants built the picturesque little town of Clamecy, the Bruges of the Morvan; and here on January 29, 1866, Romain Rolland was born.

Around Clamecy there still lingers the memory of the old German woodlanders and their craft; for the railway sidings, encumbered with piles of the tiny bundles of faggots which are so indispensable to the Parisian housekeeper, seem to show that the Morvanais of to-day earns his livelihood in the manner of his German forbears. Their memory, too, the Morvanais perpetuates in those Teutonic features of physique and disposition which cause him to appear curiously un-French. In character he is more reserved, in manner less animated, in stature taller, in complexion fairer, than the average French type.

All these characteristics M. Rolland has inherited from ancestors on both sides, who for generations have been natives of the Morvan, of Burgundy, or of another border province, Franche Comté. From them he has derived the high forehead, the dreamy far-away look in the blue-grey eyes, and the quiet and reserved manner which suggest German idealism rather than the actuality and alertness of the modern Frenchman. From them he received that passion for music which in his boyhood, had his parents encouraged it, would have led him to choose a musician's career. To them he owes also certain literary and mental characteristics, a rhapsodical manner, a deep sense of life's tragedy, and a tendency to dwell on the mystic and moral rather than on the purely artistic and intellectual interpretation of things.

Un-French as he is in so many ways, it is not surprising to find M. Rolland confessing[1] that often in the presence of his countrymen there comes over him a feeling of aloofness as if he belonged to some foreign race. It is natural, too, that the so-called French writers with whom M. Rolland has most in common, J. J. Rousseau and Edouard Rod, should both be of Swiss extraction. In this fact

[1] In *Dans la Maison*, p. 95.

one seems to catch an echo of distant days, when there was a close connexion between Burgundy and Switzerland and when Burgundian dukes ruled over Swiss cantons.

His inherited Teutonism has enabled M. Rolland to penetrate deep into the soul of the German people, to comprehend and to describe with power and insight the faults and the virtues of this nation. But not of this nation only, for it would be highly unjust to M. Rolland to represent him as merely interested in Germany; with equal insight and impartiality he has seized and portrayed the soul of his own people, and of those other Swiss and Italian peoples among whom he has dwelt from time to time. Superb flashes of racial psychology illuminate the pages of *Jean Christophe*. Here is one of them from *La Révolte*:[1] "It is not legislators and statesmen, priests and philosophers, who transform the souls of races and clothe them in a new nature: it is centuries of misfortune and trial which temper for life those nations which desire to live."[2]

[1] The fourth volume of *Jean Christophe*, p. 34.

[2] To this statement the corruption of the German people by forty-four years of material prosperity presents a striking corollary.

M. Rolland, far from confining his sympathies to any one nation, has the faculty of thinking Europeanly, if one may use such a word. He, like his own Jean Christophe, "has a European mind."

He owes it not only to his Burgundian origin but to the cosmopolitan influences which have moulded him from his youth upward: his residence in the two most cosmopolitan cities of the world, Paris and Rome, his travels through Europe, his study of foreign writers, his passion for foreign art, especially for German music, his friendship with many distinguished foreigners, notably with an accomplished German lady, Malwida von Meysenbug.

It was in early youth that M. Rolland came to Paris. His school-days at Clamecy being over, Madame Rolland, who had discerned in her son gifts far above the average, persuaded his father to abandon his notary's practice at Clamecy and to migrate with his family to the capital. Here, in what he has described as *ce grand salon d'hotel cosmopolite qu'est devenu le Tout Paris,*[1]

[1] The fifth volume of *Jean Christophe, La Foire sur la Place,* 221.

Romain Rolland soon came under foreign influences. It was in Paris that when he was still a young Lycéen at Louis-le-Grand, he fell under the spell of Wagner's music. One of the most thrilling emotions of his boyhood, Wagner has remained one of the guiding passions of his later years. *Chez le vieux Pasdeloup* in the Cirque d'Hiver, Rolland tells us, he was first initiated into this wondrous world of sound. The hall was crowded, its atmosphere close and oppressive, the benches hard and narrow, but at the very first notes all this discomfort was forgotten. "With what a strange magical intoxication did this music fill me!" he writes. "Everything in it seemed mysterious, orchestration, rhythm, subject, all that wild poetry of the remote middle age and of the legends of the barbarians, and the obscure ferment of hidden anguish and desire. I did not understand it. How could I? . . . I felt myself carried away by superhuman passion. . . . It seemed as if my child's heart had been torn from me and I had been given the heart of a hero. Thus was Jean Christophe to feel when, with flaming cheeks, laughing and trembling all over at once, he heard for the first time this marvellous music."[1]

Music, and Wagner's music especially, is for M. Rolland a great wellspring of inspiration. "Art," he writes, "is as inexhaustible as life. Nothing makes one realize it better than the ocean of music which fills the centuries." He himself admits that his mentality is a musician's. Certain passages in his work resemble some great symphony.

At Louis-le-Grand Rolland prepared for l'Ecole Normale Supérieure, which he entered in 1886. That great College was just then in a period of seething intellectual life, of which Tolstoy was the guide and philosopher. Melchior de Voguë in his *Roman Russe* had revealed Tolstoy to the Western world; and eight of his works had recently appeared in French. To the students at l'École Normale those writings of Tolstoy opened up a new universe. "Students of most divergent ideas were alike inspired by him," writes Rolland,[2] "ironical realists like the philosopher Georges Dumas, poets consumed with a passion for the Italian Renaissance like Suarés, devotees of the classical tradition, followers of Stendhal,

[1] *La Révolte*, p. 30.

[2] *Vie de Tolstoy.*

admirers of Wagner, atheists, mystics. Many were the discussions and disputes which arose between these rival schools of thought. Yet for a few months enthusiasm for Tolstoy united almost all of us. We all admired him for different reasons, for in Tolstoy's work each one found himself."

The life of Tolstoy, which, on the great teacher's death, Romain Rolland was to write, was to disclose the peculiar fascination possessed for him by Tolstoy's life and doctrine. It was the Slav's melancholy, the moralist's zeal, and the constant strife in the man's soul between voluptuousness and ascetism, between love and truth, between fact and ideal, that rendered him so sympathetic to Romain Rolland. "For Tolstoy, as," writes Rolland, "for all who are not content with mediocrity of soul, life is a perpetual battle." For Rolland this battle began early. It was waged between the various forces of his temperament; especially sharp for him has the conflict ever been between the inward and the outward man, between the spirit all fire and ardour, aglow with the blessedness of living, soaring into the realm of high heroism, and the physical body, frail and weak, threatened by a thousand ills and well nigh consumed by the fire of the spirit. Like one of Charlotte Brontë's characters, Rolland's soul "has more of will and ambition than his body of fibre and muscle." For M. Rolland it is not ideas but temperaments which constitute the differences between men; and for him the only possible classification of humanity is into those who are healthy and those who are not. That to the latter class M. Rolland belongs is sometimes too obvious in his works; for, while they ever reveal that deep comprehension of and sympathy with human woe which is alone vouchsafed to those who have drunk of the Fountain of Tears, they occasionally display an acrimony verging on peevishness which is characteristic of the invalid.

Yet it has never been M. Rolland's habit to dwell on his own sufferings, but rather to turn from them and to seek consolation in the nobility and greatness of fellow sufferers. From boyhood he has been a hero-worshipper. Beethoven, then Michael Angelo and now Tolstoy were his heroes. And in the likeness of these great spirits, souls limited by circumstance and passion and the bonds of inheritance, beaten by the waves of the spirit, Rolland was to create for himself a hero after his own heart, a Jean Christophe, such a being as Rolland himself would wish to be, all radiant with health and vigour, rejoicing in Herculean strength, exulting in the joy of living, capable of bitter tears, but also of loud ringing laughter, which echoes cheerfully through the ten volumes which tell the story of his life.

Another influence, foreign, too, be it noticed, which moulded Romain Rolland's genius, was that of Shakespeare. To a mind so philosophic yet withal so artistic as Rolland's it was natural that our great dramatist should make a strong appeal. "Of all artists Shakespeare is he whom from childhood I have most constantly preferred," writes Rolland. And it is no less natural that among Shakespeare's plays *Hamlet* should be Rolland's favourite. To Jean Christophe, amidst the doubts and troubles of his turbulent adolescence, this great tragedy was ever to be peculiarly dear.[1]

No criticism of Romain Rolland is more

[1] *La Révolte*, III.

unjust than that of certain critics who describe him as the enemy of the past.[1] On the contrary, history has ever been one of his favourite studies. "I have made it my daily bread," he writes, "I have lived as much in the past as in the present."[2] In history he specialized at l'École Normale. There he attended the lectures of that distinguished historian, Gabriel Monod, the pupil and friend of Michelet, who was later to become editor of *La Revue Historique*. M. Monod, speedily recognizing his pupil's talent, invited him to his home at Versailles; and there the young Normalien found himself in a circle at once select and cosmopolitan. Monod himself was one of the broadest-minded of men. A stalwart fighter against anti-Semitism, he was to be one of the heroes of the pro-Dreyfus campaign.

Some of the most distinguished members of M. Monod's circle were Jews; and in this *milieu* Rolland, whose interest in the Jews had already been aroused by his passion for Beethoven's music and his admiration of

[1] Notably M. Paul Souday, critic of *Le Temps*. "M. Romain Rolland est pour le passé un ennemi personnel."

[2] Preface to *Théatre du Peuple*, ed. 1913.

Spinosa's philosophy, began to study the Israelites as a race, marvelling at the wonderful part, at times second only to that of Greece, which the Jewish spirit has played in the evolution of human culture. There is hardly a volume of *Jean Christophe* which does not contain some masterly study of an Israelitish type. "As an incentive to action and an abundant source of life, the Jewish influence acts as a powerful ferment in modern society," writes Rolland.[1] "However wildly they may act, their clearness of thought and common sense never completely forsake them."[2]

It was in the Monod's home at Versailles that Romain Rolland made a friend, a German lady, who, for the next few years, was to play an important part in his life. Madame Monod was Russian by birth, the daughter of the famous Russian Nihilist, Alexander Herzen; and Madame Monod's mother by adoption was a distinguished German lady, Malwida von Meysenbug, herself a revolutionary, who had been compelled to flee from Germany and

[1] "Ils y sont un ferment d'action, un levain de vie." *Antoinette*, sixth volume of *Jean Christophe*, p. 150.

[2] *Dans la Maison*, seventh volume of *Jean Christophe*, p. 132.

take refuge in London during the troubles of '48.

Fräulein von Meysenbug was accustomed to spend her summers with her adopted daughter at Versailles. And there between this German lady, of threescore years and ten, and the young French student of three and twenty there sprang up a friendship which to Rolland has remained one of the most delightful memories of these early years. This friendship, begun at Versailles, was continued at Rome. For thither, on completing his course at l'École Normale, Rolland went to study for two years in the French School of History and Archæology, in the Palazzo Farnese. Malwida von Meysenbug had for some years spent her winters in Rome in a flat in the Via Polveria, near the Coliseum. There the young Rolland spent many happy hours. It had been his musical gift which had aroused Malwida's interest in him. But soon she discovered in her young friend much to attract her besides music. Between these two souls there was an affinity which nullified differences of age and race. In Rolland Malwida found the same yearning for the ideal, the same striving after the noblest and best, the same scorn for the commonplace and trivial, the same courage in battling for the freedom of the individual which had always filled her own soul.

Her life had been strenuous and eventful. As a German refugee in London, she had lived in a lodging-house at St. John's Wood, where she supported herself by teaching and translation. Among her friends at that time were Mazzini, Garibaldi, Wagner, Louis Blanc, and Richard Cobden. On her return to Germany she had lived at Bayreuth in order to be near Wagner and to hear his music. She was then taking charge of Alexander Herzen's three daughters. The youngest, Olga, whom Malwida had adopted, married Gabriel Monod. After this event Malwida began to spend her winters in Rome, where her salon was frequented by some of the most illustrious and progressive leaders of artistic and literary Europe, by Ibsen, Nietzsche, and Liszt, to mention only three of the most famous.

During Rolland's two years[1] in Rome, he and Malwida were constantly together. In her Memoirs[2] she frequently mentions him, telling how they made excursions or went to

[1] 1890–2. [2] *Der Lebensabend einer Idealisten, passim.*

the theatre together, and how after the day's ramble they would return to her flat, where Rolland at her piano, during long blissful hours, would employ for his aged friend's delectation his wonderful musical talent, causing the waves of harmony to roll gloriously through her soul. One may catch an echo of these Roman evenings in that scene of *Jean Christophe*, where the young musician plays to his enthusiastic friend and admirer, the venerable Schulz.[1]

"He sat down to the piano and played—as he could play when he had some one near him whom he loved. . . . The old man was in ecstasy. Seated near Christophe, he kept his eyes fixed upon him and held his breath. . . . An hour passed: Christophe was still playing. They had not exchanged a word. When Christophe had finished, neither one nor the other spoke. There was perfect silence: the house and the street slept. Christophe turned round and saw the old man in tears. He rose and kissed him. They talked in low tones, in the calm of the night. The only sound was the faint ticking of a clock in the next room. Schulz spoke softly,

[1] *La Révolte*, p. 267.

with his hands clasped and his body bent forward. In reply to Christophe's questions, he told him of his life and of his sorrows."

Thus Rolland and Malwida must have talked.

Malwida, born in 1816, was then seventy-three, Rolland twenty-three.

She must have told him the thrilling story of her life; and we know from her Memoirs that they did not hesitate to discuss those fundamental problems which for years had been agitating Rolland's mind. Both the friends were profoundly religious, both had found a solution of their doubts and difficulties in a vague deism, which for Rolland was tinged with pantheism. This faith Rolland, the year before he came to Rome, had confessed in a philosophical essay, hitherto unpublished, entitled *Credo quia verum*. After five years of spiritual anguish, Rolland had discovered what seemed to him a satisfying proof of his faith, his being and his God. From this moment he renounced metaphysics! "I have reached a basis [1] of certitude," he writes, "and I refuse to subject it to questioning. Now that the

[1] See Paul Seippel, *Romain Rolland, L'Homme et l'Œuvre*.

ground is firm beneath me, I will walk and I will create." Romain Rolland has kept his word. The credo of his youth has sufficed for him until now. Yet he does not regard it as altogether final, and there are signs that in the future he may subject it to the test of science and even of metaphysics.

Christianity with its glorification of pain and sorrow was a favourite topic of these Roman talks. Malwida and Rolland were far from being orthodox Christians. To the latter Christianity seemed pessimism, "an odour[1] bitter and intoxicating," not to succumb to which he sometimes had been forced to make a violent effort. The Christian's God, the Christian's eternal life, seemed to him the refuge of those who have failed in this mortal life; the Christian's faith was but a lack of faith in life, of faith in the future, of faith in oneself, a lack of courage and a lack of joy. Yet to such a mystical mind as Rolland's, "the wailings of Christians which for nineteen centuries have filled the Western world" were not without their appeal. Rolland, like his fellow Burgundian, Lamartine, adores melancholy wherever it finds it. Christian

[1] *Vie de Michel Ange*, p. 11.

melancholy he cannot but admire. Of Christians he writes : " You sadden the world, but you beautify it. The world would be the poorer without your sorrow. . . . Blessed be joy, blessed also be sadness. They are sisters and they are saints. They forget the world and fill great souls. They are strength, they are life, they are God. He who loves not both loves neither."

Poles asunder in thought and in manner as are Romain Rolland and Anatole France, yet they have one point in common ; they believe that to human well-being darkness and light both contribute. " In the midst of universal happiness what would become of devotion and sacrifice ? " asks Anatole France. " Can one conceive of virtue without vice, of love without hate, of beauty without ugliness ? That the earth is habitable and life livable is due to evil and to suffering. Wherefore we should not be too hard on the Devil. He is a great artist and a great scientist. He has made at least one half of the world, and this half so closely fitted into the other that it cannot be injured without the other's hurt." [1]

Yet it was not melancholy that appealed

[1] *Le Jardin d'Epicure*, p. 88.

most to Romain Rolland during those two glad years beneath the Italian sky. Amidst the grandeur and the glory that was Rome it was an intense delight to Malwida to watch her young friend's genius blooming freely in joy and gladness like a flower transplanted back to its natural soil.

Rome captivated Rolland as she was to captivate his hero Christophe; and it is his own experience he is describing when he tells how Christophe first came upon the Forum red in the setting sun, beneath the crumbling arches of the Palatine standing out against a background of deep azure, and how the Roman light, the hanging gardens, the Campagna, girding like a golden scarf the sunlit sea, revealed to him the secret of this enchanted land.[1] To the heavenly light of the Italian sky, *lumière, sang du monde qui coule dans l'espace comme un fleuve de vie*, Rolland in these pages sings a truly Miltonic hymn of praise.

In his Roman historical studies the period in which Romain Rolland specialized was the Italian Renaissance, the period of his hero, Michael Angelo. Already before journey-

[1] The tenth volume of *Jean Christophe, La Nouvelle Journée*, pp. 39, 27 and *passim*.

ing south he had written, under the influence of Shakespeare's historical plays, three dramas, *Orsino*, *Les Baglioni*, and *Le Siège de Mantoue*, dealing with this period. These early works he read to Malwida, who found them so full of promise that she looked to her young friend to resuscitate the historical drama in France. Mounet Sully also had read the *Orsino*, and if he could have had his wish it would have been produced at the Comédie Française. None of these prentice pieces or those on classical themes, *Niobe*, *Caligula*, and *Empedocle*, which last was written in Rome, have hitherto been published.[1]

All too swiftly fled Rolland's two glorious years in Rome, and all too soon came the time for him to return to Paris and weave his strands into the great loom of life. Before they parted he and Malwida made a little tour together. They met at Venice, wandered through Umbria and reached Bayreuth in time for the Wagner Festival. At Bayreuth they stood side by side at Wagner's grave and together saw Parsifal. Then they bade each other farewell. Malwida's heart was

[1] *Jeanne de Piennes* was another historical play written about this time.

full of thankfulness for the wealth of music and poetry her friend had revealed to her, but she was oppressed with the sad presentiment of age who beholds youth go forth to meet those sorrows and deceptions which must inevitably attend the enthusiastic idealist.

Her gratitude to Rolland she expressed in the following verses inscribed in her Memoirs :

Armer wurde die Welt und immer armer und armer,
Ode und Einsamkeit wurde es rings um mich her
Wenn der Frühling wieder aufs neue erschienen,
Frische Blüten der Flur brachten mit lacheln dem Grusz,
Schied mir ein Freund, ein Bruder, der liebe Verwandte
In die dunkele Fern, aus der keiner Zuruckkehrt.

Deine Hand wars, mein Freund, die jene Klange entlockte
Und mit herzlichen Dank mich dir in Freundschaft verband ;
Scheid ich, folgt nun dein Bild vereint mit jenen Groszen,
Von Harmonien umtont, in die Ferne mir nach.

Rolland went on his way, his soul soothed and brightened by Malwida's noble calmness and dignified serenity. Despite the sadness and suffering of her life, despite her experience of human baseness, she had lost none of her youth. For Rolland she seemed to harmonize with Rome and to help him to taste to the full the *sens auguste et apaisant* of the Holy City.

In Paris, Romain Rolland remained in touch with the chief currents of European thought. He continued to frequent cosmopolitan circles and to visit at frequent intervals Germany, Italy, and Switzerland. It would be difficult to exaggerate the importance of the influence which these residences abroad never failed to exercise on Rolland's work.[1] After his marriage in 1892 he was entrusted with an official mission which took him back to Italy. There he collected material for his thesis: *L'Histoire de l'Opéra en Europe avant Lulli et Scarlatti,* which he maintained at the Sorbonne on June 19, 1895. Two years later he returned to his old college, l'École Normale, as lecturer on the history of art. Many a young man of letters in France to-day looks back to those lectures with delight. For some, notably for the late M. Charles Péguy, editor of *Les Cahiers de la Quinzaine,*[2] and for the brothers Messieurs

[1] "Les forêts de Suisse," he writes, "ont tenu une grande place dans l'histoire de ma pensée."

[2] See *ante,* pp. 21 and *n.,* 30.

Jean and Jérôme Tharaud, they were the beginning of a close and lasting friendship with the lecturer. In 1903, M. Rolland left the École Normale for the Sorbonne, where a chair of the history of the Art of Music had been created for him. His lectures, attended by large audiences, he illustrated by playing on the piano extracts from the works under discussion. In 1910, however, M. Rolland, to whom this work had never been congenial, resigned his professorship; and since then writing has been his sole occupation. During these years Rolland had been exercising his literary gifts in the historical drama. His first published work was the play *St. Louis*, which appeared in *La Revue de Paris*, in 1896. A play in three acts, entitled *Aërt*,[1] was acted by Le Théatre de l'Œuvre in 1898, and followed by three plays on the Revolution, *Les Loups* (originally entitled *Morthuri*), *Le 14 Juillet*, and *Danton*.[2]

These plays were dedicated to the people of Paris; for Rolland was at this time possessed by the idea of founding a popular theatre.

[1] Published recently in a volume entitled *Les Tragédies de la Foi*.

[2] Since published in a volume entitled *Le Théatre de la Révolution*.

He had been encouraged in this project by a correspondence he had recently been carrying on with Tolstoy, occasioned by the master's violent attack on art in his book *Qu'est-ce que l'Art*. Tolstoy's sweeping denunciation of artists whose masterpieces were meat and drink to Rolland—Shakespeare, Beethoven, Wagner—as false geniuses, for whom men had been seized with an infatuation nothing better than those other manias, the Crusades, belief in witches, search for the philosopher's stone, and a passion for tulips which had from time to time come upon humanity, drew from Rolland a letter to which Tolstoy replied. The arrival of the master's missive in his humble student's apartment in the Montparnasse quarter of Paris marked one of the most memorable days in Rolland's career. The criticism of modern art and modern artists which this letter contained has ever since profoundly influenced Rolland's conception of life and of art. In Tolstoy's eyes modern art is but a whitened sepulchre, an immense humbug, arising from the fact that people calling themselves civilized have placed over them artists and scholars, who have become a privileged caste, parasites preying upon society. Now, according to Tolstoy everything that separates men is ugly and evil, everything that unites them beautiful and good. Henceforth art if it will be true must cease to be practised only by a privileged caste, it must return to the people.

These doctrines sank deep into Rolland's soul. They found expression in the strenuous efforts he was making to found a popular theatre. It was with this object that in 1903 he wrote a book entitled *Le Théatre du Peuple*. A theatre is being founded, he wrote, which has nothing in common with fashion or dilettantism, but which is the imperious expression of a new society, its voice and its thought, and necessarily therefore at this critical hour it becomes the weapon by which this society will attack the old, which has grown effete and corrupt.

Rolland's bitterness towards society was the natural outcome of personal experiences. During the closing years of the last century he had journeyed far into the country of sorrow, he had drunk deep of the fountain of tears. In heart and home he had suffered; cherished illusions had dropped from him, old ideals had been shattered, public events, the Dreyfus case and the Boer War, had intensified his bitterness ; l'Affaire Dreyfus had seemed to him a holy hysteria. Unlike many of his friends, Charles Péguy for example, he did not go down into the arena of battle, but, standing aloof and observing closely, he perceived the nobility mingled with baseness which characterized alike both parties in the struggle. He was therefore prepared for the bitter disillusionment which even in the hour of victory attended those heroic disinterested souls who had sacrificed themselves for an ideal.

These heroes of the Dreyfus campaign he had in mind when in the seventh volume of *Jean Christophe* (*Dans la Maison*) he described the bitter disappointment of the Dreyfusard Erlsberger and his wife. "Their hopes had been so high, their zeal for sacrifice so pure, that the victory which came, in comparison with that of which they had dreamed, seemed contemptible. For these single-minded creatures . . . the transactions of politicians, the compromises of their heroes, had been a bitter deception. They had seen their companions in the struggle, those whom they had believed animated by the same all-absorbing passion for justice as themselves, once they had conquered the enemy, rush to the *curée*, seize power, scramble for honours and places, and in their turn trample justice under foot. Only a small group of them remained who were true to their faith; but these were poor, isolated, rejected by all parties and rejecting all; returning into obscurity, separated one from the other, dimmed by sadness, victims of neurasthenia, having lost hope in everything, disgusted with mankind and weary of life."

When Rolland wrote these lines he was thinking of Colonel Picquart, whose career then seemed to have been ruined by his love of justice; he was thinking of his own friend, the noble Charles Péguy, and of the Jew Bernard Lazare, to whose memory Péguy has consecrated some of the most eloquent pages of his deeply moving book *Notre Jeunesse*. Bernard Lazare died of l'Affaire Dreyfus. "Even to-day," wrote Rolland in 1901, "we have just beheld two of the purest aspirations towards justice and liberty, Colonel Picquart and the Boer people." [1]

[1] *Vie de Beethoven*, VI.

In France at this time there was many a noble, sympathetic, tender-hearted soul to whom England's treatment of the Boer Republic was a blow far heavier than any personal sorrow; for they had come to regard our Government as the friend of oppressed and struggling nationalities, as the personification of the humanitarian spirit; and when, at the bidding of a few financiers, as it seemed to them, England deprived these people of their freedom, our nation fell from her high estate, righteousness and truth forsook the world. French writers, notably Rolland's two young friends and former pupils at l'École Normale, Jean and Jérôme Tharaud, in their novel *Dingley l'Illustre Ecrivain*, with ruthless irony wrote of the jingoism then rampant in this country. Rolland himself, in his play *Le Temps Viendra*,[1] which represents a noble, patriotic, God-fearing Boer family, whose home is invaded by British soldiers, uttered a protest not against this war only but against war in general. One of the characters in the play, Clifford, an English general, is made to say to a comrade: "There was a time when I exulted in war;

[1] *Les Cahiers de la Quinzaine*, 1903.

in my youth I found happiness in it. But in our day, Miles, at our age, a thoughtful man cannot fail to realize that there is something archaic in war and to blush at having anything to do with it."

In the intervals of his teaching career M. Rolland had been chiefly occupied with the theatre. With the dawn of the new century he began to give literary expression, in a series of biographies, to the hero worship of his early years. "Great souls," he wrote, "are like high mountain tops, buffeted by winds, enveloped by clouds, but surrounded by air stronger and purer than the stifling atmosphere of every day life." "Open the windows and let in the fresh air. Let us breathe the breath of heroes," cried Rolland. Like his own Christophe, he was living the life of a visionary. "Everything he saw and heard evoked within him beings and things different from those which were actually around him. He had only to let himself go and he found everywhere the life of his heroes." By heroes he means, so he tells us, not those who have conquered through physical or mental force, but those whose hearts are great, "those who do what they can."

The French painter, Millet, is the subject of the first of these biographies. It appeared, strange to say, in English ; and the original French has not, as far as I know, yet been published. But it is not as the biographer of Millet or of Handel, whose life he wrote for Alcan's Masters of Music series, that M. Rolland is best known. These works are little read in comparison with those three masterpieces of biography, the lives of Beethoven, Michael Angelo, and Tolstoy. These Promethean souls, giants of music, art, and literature, had ever occupied the first rank among Rolland's heroes. Men of vehement passions were they all. "Unsatisfied earthly passion," Malwida used to say, "is the price the gods make men pay for genius." Men of conflict were they too, and not always victorious in their battles.

In his fight with weakness of will Michael Angelo was often worsted. He was ever beset by a Hamlet-like contradiction between imperious passions and a will which willed not. The might of his genius his body and soul seemed too weak to hold. Michael Angelo never attained to the serene joy of Beethoven. How different is the worn harassed look, preserved for us in the Louvre bust of this great artist, from the calm joy which towards the close of his life, we read, gladdened the countenance of the deaf musician, Beethoven. Michael Angelo spent his last years waiting for death to deliver him from human woe. He believed happiness to be alone attainable beyond the grave. In another world he thought to cast off the melancholy which embittered his life here below. It was in the shadow of this Christian gloom that Rolland wrote of the wailings of Christians which had filled our Western world for nineteen centuries.

Tolstoy, like Michael Angelo, strove ever after peace but found it not. The picture of his strenuous soul Rolland has painted with consummate power and tenderest sympathy, for with Tolstoy more than with either of his other heroes Rolland has most affinity. With many of the struggles which rent Tolstoy's soul Rolland was himself familiar. He knew what it was to stand hesitating and perplexed before the rival claims of truth and love. "How often," he writes, "does an artist, an artist who is worthy of the name and who is conscious of the glorious yet terrible power of the written word—how often, when about to express some truth, does he not feel himself torn asunder! That truth, wholesome and virile, necessary in the midst of modern falsehood and the lies of civilization, that vital truth, seems to him like the very air he breathes. And then he perceives that there exist lungs for which this air is too strong, beings enfeebled by civilization or weak simply through kindness of heart! Ought one to ignore their weakness and show them the truth which will be their death? Is there not above and beyond a higher truth which, as Tolstoy says, is subject to love? Can one consent then to lull men with consoling lies, like Peer Gynt amusing his old dying mother with fairy tales? Society is ever confronted by this dilemma: the alternative of truth or love. Its common solution of the problem is the sacrifice of both."

The anguish of unsolved problems, the perplexity of Tolstoy's last years and his final sacrifice of love to truth, M. Rolland describes forcibly, lovingly, and with that deep comprehension of the human heart which was already leading him so powerfully to portray the heart-searchings of his own Jean Christophe. For the life of Tolstoy, written in

1911, had been preceded by eight volumes of *Jean Christophe*, and in this year Rolland was engaged on the ninth volume, *Le Buisson Ardent*.[1]

In the opinion of many of M. Rolland's readers his *Life of Beethoven* is his most typical piece of work. Palpitating with life, masterpieces of psychological insight and powerful expression as are all three biographies, the *Life of Beethoven* is even finer, more sympathetic and characteristic of Rolland's genius than the other two.

In this book, reflected in the lucid mirror of the author's mind, is the living image of a great, a gifted, a generous, and a much-tried soul.

The first of all the virtues is joy, wrote Rolland. Joy realized through suffering is the note of this book. Rolland's heroes were all men of sorrows, but Beethoven was the most heavily afflicted; poverty, loneliness, and deafness, that to a musician the most terrible of all afflictions, came upon him.

It is indeed to the sorrowful that this book is addressed. "For who among us,"

[1] For the close connexion between these biographies and various volumes of *Jean Christophe*, see post, pp. 134, 168.

asks Rolland, "has not known sorrow?" "Yet Beethoven's sorrows," he writes, "should teach us not to complain too loudly, for never is life greater, more fruitful nor more truly happy than in suffering." "Dear Beethoven,"[1] he exclaims, in the last chapter of this book, "many have praised his greatness as an artist, but, much more than the greatest of musicians, he is among modern artists the greatest inspirer of heroism, the best and dearest friend of those who strive and suffer. When we are saddened by the world's misery, he comes to us as he came to a mother mourning for her child, and with his music, his plaintive hymn of resignation chased away her tears. Wearied by perpetual and useless battling against the mediocrity of vice and virtue, how unspeakably refreshing is it to bathe in this ocean of will and faith."

The joy for which Beethoven had vainly longed all his life came to him at length and at a time when to the world he seemed most afflicted. One who saw him in 1826 says that his expression had become so glad as to be almost jovial. It was at this time that in the Ninth Symphony he composed his hymn

[1] *Vie de Beethoven*, pp. 76, 7.

to Joy. The advent of this theme, writes Rolland, after a sudden silence, clothes it in an atmosphere mysterious and divine. Indeed, it is like the descent of a god, joy coming down from heaven, clothed in supernatural calm, with its soft breath caressing sorrow.[1] Henceforth Beethoven rose superior to his sorrows. Three years after the first public performance of the Ninth Symphony he died. Among his last words were these: "I am patient, for I remember that every evil is attended with some good."

These biographies are great soul dramas. In unity of conception, in power of expression, and in psychological insight they rank far above those of the author's works which are couched in dramatic form. As a dramatist, M. Rolland has never achieved brilliant success, as a biographer he is among the first of contemporary writers; and one is glad to learn that he has in preparation the *Life of Mozart*, and a psychological study of Handel.

The Beethoven, the Michael Angelo, and the Tolstoy, as well as most of M. Rolland's plays, all appeared originally in *Les Cahiers de*

[1] *Vie de Beethoven*, p. 64.

la Quinzaine. It would hardly be an exaggeration to say that among the younger generation of French writers every one who counts may be found represented in some number of *Les Cahiers.* A dominant note in the ante-War period of French literature will ever remain the Thursday afternoons at *Les Cahiers,* when in the cramped little office in the Rue de la Sorbonne, the editor, Charles Péguy, used to gather round him his collaborators—all the most promising young spirits of Paris—Romain Rolland, the Tharauds, Pierre Mille, Georges Sorel, Daniel Halèvy, and many others. Now the closed shutters of No. 8 Rue de la Sorbonne signify more than the death of a literary journal, more even than the heroic passing of its gifted founder and editor: they indicate the close of a literary epoch.

It was the appearance, wrote M. Péguy, of the Life of Beethoven in *Les Cahiers* in 1903, that first made the literary fortune of this publication. The Michael Angelo appeared in July and October 1906, and the Tolstoy in March 1911. In *Les Cahiers* also were appearing the various volumes of *Jean Christophe,* the first, *L'Aube,* in 1904.

From 1904 until 1912, when the final volume of his novel appeared, M. Rolland was absorbed in the creation of his hero. "*J'ai bati patiemment ce héro,*" he writes.

In the ideal world of Jean Christophe he lived and moved and had his being. The biographies may be regarded as studies for certain phases of Jean Christophe's life. The *Beethoven* corresponds with *L'Aube* and *Le Matin,* the *Michel Ange* with the end of *L'Adolescent, La Révolte* and *La Foire sur la Place,* the *Tolstoi* with *Le Buisson Ardent. La Nouvelle Journée,* we are told, was written under the inspiration of Goethe, whose life M. Rolland has yet to write.

The various pages of *Jean Christophe* first saw the light in different parts of Europe. Many of them were written in the author's Paris home, the simple somewhat austere rooms in a house on the Boulevard Montparnasse, not unlike that described in *Dans la Maison* as occupied by Jean Christophe and his friend Olivier. Others, parts of *L'Aube* for example, were written under the inspiration of, if not during, M. Rolland's visit to Bonn for the Beethoven celebration of 1901, for it is not difficult to identify with Beethoven's birthplace the Rhenish town in which Christophe was born and in which he spent his childhood. For many years M. Rolland has been accustomed to spend some part of the summer in Switzerland, and there much of *Jean Christophe* was written. When his great work was completed, M. Rolland intended to continue his travels, for he believes that one can only comprehend the various phases of society by constantly changing one's point of view. In accordance with his cosmopolitan ideas, M. Rolland has, since the beginning of the War, continued to reside in a neutral country, in Switzerland. Endeavouring by his articles in the *Journal de Genève*, to calm the fury of national hatreds, he has, alas! merely succeeded in rendering himself unpopular both in France and in Germany. Nevertheless how completely false is the charge of pro-Germanism brought against him in France is proved by the eloquent pages he has recently contributed to the first number of a new publication, *Les Cahiers Vaudois*, which appears at Lausanne. Here he admits the failure of his efforts to inspire German intellectuals with any realization of or regret for atrocities committed. Such a failure must be one of the bitterest disappointments to the author of *Jean Christophe,* that heroic attempt to blend the spirits of France and of Germany.

JEAN CHRISTOPHE

JEAN CHRISTOPHE

So far, it is *Jean Christophe* alone that entitles M. Romain Rolland to rank as a novelist. Throughout Europe his ten-volume novel has probably been more widely read and more eagerly discussed than any other novel of our time. Indeed, the literary world of Western Europe is divided into two camps, the friends and the enemies of *Jean Christophe*. *Jean Christophe*'s friends find in these ten volumes one of the most significant works of the day, the great prose epic of a human soul tossed on the billows of passion, buffeted by the waves of circumstance, and moving across a stage which presents in one vast panorama the culture of modern Europe. *Jean Christophe*'s enemies stand aghast, lost in bewilderment at this " cauldron of emotions and speculations burning and boiling over in profuse confusion." What are they to call this colossal, formless ebullition, they ask ? Is it a history, is it a prose epic ?

It surely cannot be a novel. To these critics Romain Rolland has replied in his preface to the seventh volume of *Jean Christophe*.

"It is clear," he writes, "that I have never aspired to write a novel. . . . What is this work then? Is it a poem? Why must you all call it by any name? When you see a man, do you ask whether he be a novel or a poem? It is a man that I am creating. A man's life refuses to be confined within the limits of any literary form."

It will be seen, therefore, that M. Rolland, like his own Jean Christophe, is *un revolté*, a rebel against the existing order including literary conventions. Those inclined to censure M. Rolland for this rebellion might remember that every forward step in the history of the world's progress has been taken by a rebel. M. Rolland at present stands alone; he belongs to no school; he has no imitators. It would be as impossible to imitate Rolland as to imitate Carlyle. Rolland and his work stand alone. It may be that he foreshadows a new France, a new literature in which life not art shall be the dominant note.

"Jean Christophe has always appeared to

me as a river," wrote M. Rolland. And to readers of *Jean Christophe* the hero does indeed seem like some Greek personification of a mighty stream flowing into the sea of eternity. He begins with all the vehemence and the turbulence and the turgidity of the water of the German river, on the banks of which he was born, the Vater Rein as it tumbles down the rocks at Schaffhausen; but in the progress of his career, and from his contact with the French spirit, Jean Christophe acquires the lucidity and the serenity of the French river, the limpid Seine, on the banks of which he ended his course.

M. Rolland is not a writer who stands aloof from his work. On the contrary it absorbs him. Writing, shortly before the War, to a friend in Paris[1] of the new novel on which he is now engaged he said: "I have been writing my new novel with great joy and ardour, my hero has so completely absorbed me that I seem to be incarnated in him." And thus for eight years was M. Rolland incarnated in Jean Christophe. The first volume appeared in *Les*

[1] The publisher, M. Edouard Champion.

Cahiers de la Quinzaine, in February 1904. On June 26, 1912, he wrote from Baveno: "I have finished my last volume, *La Nouvelle Journée*, I feel glad and free." But ten years before the appearance of the first Cahier of *Jean Christophe*, M. Rolland had conceived the plan of the whole work; and earlier still, when a student at l'École Normale, the idea had come to him that one day he would write the history of a musician, a modern Beethoven. "Before penning the first line of the work," he wrote, "I had borne it within me for years. It was not until I had planned every step of his way that Christophe began his course." Yet from this course, which his creator had mapped out for him, Jean Christophe deviates considerably. He deviates so often that the story of his life includes wellnigh every aspect of human existence. There is everything in *Jean Christophe*, and one wonders what else the author has left to write about.

The first lines of the book were penned in 1897. By 1900 there existed a few pages of the first volume of *L'Aube* and one or two chapters of the fifth volume of *La Foire sur la Place*; by 1902 M. Rolland had sketched the outline of his last volume but one, *Le Buisson Ardent*.

Sincerity is the dominant note of *Jean Christophe*; never was novel more completely the expression of the writer's soul. "I was lonely," he writes. "Like so many others in France I felt myself in a hostile moral world, in which it was impossible to breathe. I was stifled. I wanted to protest against this unhealthy civilization, against the corrupt thought of the so-called elect. I wanted to say to this elect, 'you lie, you don't represent France.' In order to do this I needed a hero pure of heart and eye, whose wellnigh incorruptible soul should give him the right to speak with a voice which should make itself heard."

It is the tragedy, not of a life only but of a whole generation, that M. Rolland has revealed in *Jean Christophe*. And no student of modern thought can afford to neglect this book. He will not read it for its style. M. Rolland makes light of style. Jean Christophe advises his literary friend Olivier not to trouble about the words he uses, not to distinguish between words noble and words vulgar, nor to be concerned about the purity of his style, but to say what he has to say, to think what he thinks, to feel what he feels, to express himself in his work."[1] This is what Romain Rolland does. He does not "write." He scorns a polished, august writer, like Anatole France, whom he accuses of writing for the sake of writing; Rolland boasts that he writes because he has something to say. His great novel has all the inequalities and the blemishes of life; parts of it appear jagged and unfinished, like the unhewn marble which so often forms a part of Rodin's statues. *L'Homme Qui Marche*, the title of one of Rodin's most famous works, is the description Rolland has himself given of *Jean Christophe*. Rolland's work, like the sculpture of his great compatriot, abounds in life, is pregnant with vitality; and sometimes that very vitality creates a harmonious style of its own. Passages of this novel rise to heights of purest lyricism; for M. Rolland is a poet and a poet of the heart. But he is also a poet of the Miltonic order, for he is a great hater. Rolland admires Milton because he hated with all his heart, because he fought with the pen as the Ironsides fought

[1] *Les Amies*, p. 99.

with the sword ; and the Hebrew prophets who inspired Milton he admires for the same reason. In the frequent imprecations, the rhapsodies, the denunciations of Jean Christophe, there is much to remind one of Milton's turbulent prose.

From a purely literary point of view the finest volumes of the novel are the two first, *L'Aube* and *Le Matin.* They tell of Christophe's infancy and childhood passed in a Rhenish town, which has been identified with Bonn.

The childlessness of which Taine in his history of English literature accuses the literature of his own country no longer exists. French fiction of to-day abounds in minute and careful studies of child life. Yet nowhere shall we find a more real and fascinating picture of childhood than in *L'Aube.*

Few writers introduce their characters at quite so early an age as Romain Rolland. For Christophe appears in his cradle. Here we see him harassed by baby fears, convulsed by baby pains, haunted by "the hallucinations of a brain which has barely emerged from chaos." His little being experiences all the primitive human emotions. Intoxicated with the sense of his own strength his tiny mind and body are in a state of perpetual motion. Like a little salamander he dances in the flame. Already in babyhood he has the ear of a musician. He stops crying at the sound of church bells; he is moved to the depths of his little soul by the old ditties with which his mother lulls him to sleep.

But soon these simple joys of infancy are clouded by the sadness of childhood in a home where the father is a drunkard, and the mother forced to drudge pitifully in order to keep a roof over her children's heads. In such a home the responsibilities of life fall early on Christophe. When himself still little more than a baby he is set to mind his two baby brothers while his mother goes out to work in order to supplement her husband's earnings squandered at the wine-shop. Then Christophe's father, who is a musician, discovers his son's musical gifts and brings him out as an infant prodigy. Christophe, early in his teens, finds himself the breadwinner of the family. Yet his existence is not all misery. Simple joys still gladden his heart; and one of his greatest pleasures is to wander through the fields with his uncle Gottfried, a poor pedlar, half-witted the world calls him, for he is but slenderly endowed with this world's wisdom. Yet his nature is richly stored with true poetry, deep intuition and spontaneous gladness. Gottfried is a character, which Rolland's great master, Tolstoy, would have found after his own heart.

Nevertheless Christophe is a lonely child, and when at length he makes a friend of Otto, a boy of his own age, his delight knows no bounds. Without restraint or hesitation Christophe gives his heart into Otto's keeping. For a time all is rapture and enthusiasm. The passionate affection of Christophe and Otto is more like that of two boarding-school misses than of two young boys. But it all ends in disillusionment. For Otto is in reality a commonplace little snob quite unworthy of Christophe's ardent devotion. Christophe is no less unfortunate in his first love. He begins young and he continues to fall violently in love all his days. Romain Rolland is at his best when describing love episodes ; here he continues the tradition of Jean Jacques Rousseau and of his fellow Burgundian, Alphonse de Lamartine. With masterly touch, Rolland paints love's dawn in the hearts of the children —Christophe and Minna are mere children still. At first their love is wavering, uncertain, unconscious of itself or of its object, then becoming more definite it bursts forth in sudden expression, then again it hides itself behind infantile shyness, until finally in mutual comprehension it blooms into happiness and joy. But the joy is short-lived, for Minna after all was nothing but a materialistic little German *housefrau*. Her grossness, her selfishness, "her curiosity innocent only through ignorance," Rolland exposes mercilessly. Minna is the feminine type towards which he finds it hardest to be even just. She is the *femme du monde* in embryo, the rich woman who spells ruin for the artist. "Wealth is a disease," he writes, "and to woman it is more fatal than to man." In the course of this novel we shall meet with many a maturer sister of Minna, but in no case shall we find this phase of femininity more minutely studied.

Christophe, as we have said, was to fall frequently and furiously in love, to suffer bitter deception, to grieve long, to recover from his hurt, and to love anew. His passion for the beautiful Sabine is the most poetical of all his loves. Its story adorns the pages of the third volume, *L'Adolescent*. Sabine's distinguished grace is enhanced by the commonplace vulgarity of the German people, the Euler family, in whose house she lives. In contrast with Amalia, the Euler mother, who is all censoriousness and conventionality, whose slavish adherence to duty rendered virtue loathsome, and whose rampagious scrubbings to the accompaniment of perpetual chatter nearly drove Christophe mad, Sabine's languid indolence possessed an irresistible charm. It was as refreshing as a clear, limpid pool overshadowed by green branches, when one comes upon it after following the course of a noisy, turbid mountain torrent. Sabine is all stillness and serenity, "she neither strives nor cares." Every slow movement of her slender, frail form, suggests repose. Her willowy grace recalls some figure in a pre-Raphaelite picture. Like a Whistler nocturne, the loves of Sabine and Christophe pass peacefully, silently, coloured softly by neutral tints of reserve, restraint, deepening into that tragedy of the might-have-been, which we shall meet again when from Christophe's horizon vanishes regretfully the sad figure of Antoinette. Sabine dwelt with beauty.

> Beauty that must die ;
> And Joy, whose hand is ever at his lips
> Bidding adieu.

And the bliss of Sabine and Christophe was as fleeting as April sunshine : a few brief evenings seated together in silence, or low converse on the bench outside the house door, a summer excursion, the weary ache of pleasure nearly yet not quite realized, chance meetings in Sabine's tiny garden ; one of these a priceless gem of delicate poetry and idyllic grace, a pen picture like those painted by the brush of a Rossetti or a Burne-Jones ; the atmosphere is so delicate and so ethereal that it must be quoted in the original French.[1]

Sabine is seated at her house door shelling peas. Christophe, on the doorstep at her feet, gathering from amidst the folds of her dress in her lap handfuls of the green pods,

[1] *L'Adolescent*, pp. 92–3.

which he breaks, allowing the little round balls to fall into the bowl placed between Sabine's knees.

"Il regardait à terre. Il voyait les bas noirs de Sabine, qui moulaient ses chevilles et ses pieds, dont l'un sortait à demi de l'un de ses souliers. Il n'osait lever les yeux vers elle.

"L'air était lourde. Le ciel était très blanc, très bas, dans un souffle. Aucune feuille ne bougeait. Le jardin était clos de grands murs ; le monde finissait là.

"L'enfant était sortie avec une voisine. Ils étaient seuls. Ils ne disaient rien. Ils ne pouvaient plus rien dire. Sans voir, il prenait sur les genoux de Sabine d'autres poignées de petits pois ; ses doigts tremblaient en la touchant : ils rencontrèrent, au milieu des gousses fraîches et lisses, les doigts de Sabine qui tremblaient. Ils ne purent plus continuer. Ils restèrent immobiles, ne se regardant pas : elle renversée sur sa chaise, la bouche entr'ouverte, les bras pendants ; lui, assis à ses pieds adossé contre elle ; il sentait le long de son épaule et de son bras la tiédeur de la jambe de Sabine. Ils étaient haletants. Christophe appuyait ses mains contre la pierre, pour les rafraîchir : une de ses mains frola le pied de Sabine, sorti de son soulier, et resta posée sur lui, ne put se détacher. Un frisson les parcourut. Ils étaient près du vertige. La main de Christophe serrait les doigts menus du petit pied de Sabine. Sabine, moite et glacée, se penchait vers Christophe. . . .

"Des voix les arrachèrent à cette ivresse."

What sublime art is here ! In its tender simplicity, in its primitive grace, in the delicate creation of an atmosphere of passion, this scene is unsurpassed by anything in the French literature to-day, by little in the French literature of the past. Alas ! the idyll passes like a gleam of sunlight on a winter morning. Sabine fades away. Christophe returns from a journey and finds her dead.

Christophe's life was a series of violent reactions. His love for Sabine is succeeded by his love for Ada, as gross and as sensual as Sabine was refined and delicate. Yet Ada with her evil intentions was powerless to corrupt Christophe. His love for her was not wise, neither was it intelligent nor even happy, but it was not vile. Ada, realizing her powerlessness to ruin Christophe, betrays him; and thus she delivers him from her power, but not from himself. "The most dangerous part of passion is the ruins it accumulates." In Christophe's heart the death of passion had left a craving for pleasure. This craving he tries to satisfy in the company of Bohemian adventurers. In their society he yields to inherited weakness, the vice of his father comes upon him and he is in imminent danger of becoming a drunkard.

In the early pages of this, the third volume, *L'Adolescent*, Christophe had lost his faith; in the closing pages he finds it. As a boy and a youth Christophe had thought little of religion. An unconscious pantheist, he had been too religious to think much of God, for in God he lived and moved and had his being, what need therefore to believe in Him? "A noble, healthy soul, overflowing with life and strength has a thousand better things to do than to trouble about the existence or non-existence of the Deity," writes Rolland. Jesus, too, occupied but a very small space in Christophe's thoughts. Not that he didn't love Jesus; he did love Him when he thought about Him, but that was seldom. Beethoven was more sympathetic to him than Jesus. When he played the organ for mass at St. Florian's, his instrument occupied a larger place in his thoughts than the service he was accompanying. He was more religious on days when the orchestra played Bach than when it played Mendelssohn. During certain parts of the service he was in a fever of exaltation. One day a priest chanced to inquire playfully whether in these moments it was God or the music he loved. Those words sank deep into Christophe's heart. Were they true, did he love God, did he believe in God, was it possible for him to believe? Failing to answer this question for himself, he sought help from his neighbours. Did they believe, and if so, why? No one gave him a satisfactory answer. Some refused to discuss the question, others regarded it as a personal insult, others again replied that they saw no harm, and found much peace of mind in believing. The priest, to whom he had recourse, murmured a few Latin quotations and exhorted him to pray without ceasing.

Then Christophe confided his doubts and difficulties to Leonhard, a youth of his acquaintance, who was destined for the priesthood. Leonhard confessed to happiness. This young man spoke of the joy of believing. But the reasons he gave for the faith that was in him seemed to Christophe mere stereotyped phrases from books he was studying at college. They left Christophe cold. And it was his conversation with Leonhard that showed him how completely he had lost his faith. "But the loss of faith," writes Rolland, "like faith itself may be a blessing." Had Christophe never lost the old theological faith of his childhood he might never have attained to the new faith in life which comes to him at the end of this volume.

We have seen Christophe after his deliverance from Ada, moving fast along the downward road. Yet there was something that stayed him in his course. To the moral poison insinuating itself into his veins, Christophe possessed an antidote in his power of standing aloof from himself and of judging his own actions : he might seem to surrender himself entirely to his passions, yet those passions though in him were not of him. Moreover, Christophe had a strong feeling for self-preservation; he was determined not to let his spirit die. "His was a multi-personality. In his being were many souls of different worlds, different ages, different countries." And at a given signal the best of his souls rose in rebellion against those that were evil. The signal was given by Christophe's uncle, Gottfried, the poor pedlar, whom the world thought demented. But Gottfried was one of the meek to whom it was promised that they should inherit the earth. Gottfried though poor in this world's wisdom, like many another of the world's fools, was rich in spiritual insight and human sympathy. Many a happy hour had Christophe spent with him in childhood in the fields and forests listening to the crooning of Gottfried's simple peasant songs. The pedlar on his rounds was in the habit of disappearing for months and returning suddenly without word or warning. Now one evening Christophe, coming out of a tavern with brain fuddled with wine fumes, perceived Gottfried.

"Good day, Melchior," said the pedlar. Melchior was the name of Christophe's dead, drunken father. "The poor man's mind is going," thought Christophe. But, as they walked side by side, again Gottfried addressed him as Melchior. This time Christophe remonstrated, but Gottfried, looking at him straight and shaking his head, said coldly, "No, you are Melchior, I am not making any mistake." Those words, entering like iron into Christophe's soul, cured him of drunkenness. He passed a night of anguish. Then in the winter morning with Gottfried he visited Melchior's grave. As they came away he confided to his companion his doubts and difficulties, his struggles and defeats. He told him that he had ceased to believe. The pedlar smiled. "You would not live if you did not believe," he said. "Every one believes. Pray."

"Pray to what?"

Gottfried pointed to the sun appearing on the red and frosty horizon:

"Reverence the day which dawns. Think not of what will be in a year—in ten years. Think of to-day. . . . Love it, respect it, above all do not sully it, do not hinder it from bringing forth its flower. Love it when it is grey and sad like to-day. Be not troubled. See. It is winter now. Everything is asleep.

The good ground will awake. It is for us to be the good ground and as patient. Be reverent. Wait. If you are good, all will be well. If you are not, if you are weak, if you do not succeed, then you must be happy thus. For it will be because you can do no more. Then, why should you wish to do more? Why should you trouble about what you cannot do? One must do what one can."

These words, "one must do what one can," bring light into Christophe's soul. Bidding Gottfried farewell, he goes on his way, cheerfully defying the tempests of life. "Do what you will with me," he cries, "henceforth I know whither I am going."

Christophe has regained confidence in himself. In the next volume, *La Révolte*, we find him rising from despondency to the magnificent impudence of youth. He is filled with the most sanguine faith in the future, with the most arrogant contempt for the past. "For all of us," writes Rolland, "there comes a time when we must clean our slates of all traditional respect and admiration, of truth and falsehood, of everything we have not discovered for ourselves." This time had come for Christophe. Through his arrogance and self-confidence he makes enemies; he defies alike his fellow musicians in the orchestra and the Grand Duke who is his employer. Driven from his post of chief court musician, he is finally compelled to flee from the country of his birth. He escapes across the frontier into France.

With the French spirit in two widely divergent manifestations Christophe had already made acquaintance. Its frivolous, thoughtless, pleasure-loving side had been revealed to him by Corinne, the beautiful southern French actress, whose rendering of the part of Ophelia had moved Christophe to tears. This flirtation is a fleeting episode in Christophe's career. Corinne passes swiftly from its stage. But she has filled Christophe's heart with a yearning for Paris, where, so she tells the credulous musician, every one is intelligent and free, where every one thinks as he likes, does what he likes, loves or does not love without blame or criticism.

With the reverse side of the French temperament Christophe becomes acquainted in the person of a young French governess, Antoinette Jeannin. Her manner is so demure, her dress so sombre and modest, her face so serious, that Christophe would never have taken her for French. Antoinette makes three shadowy appearances on the stage of Christophe's life: they sit side by side in the theatre, they see each other in different railway trains during a brief halt at a wayside station, they catch a glimpse of one another in a crowded Parisian thoroughfare, separated by a block in the traffic; and they never meet again in the flesh. Yet in Christophe's thoughts Antoinette lives for ever; she lives at first in a sad and tender memory mingled with remorse, and with that sense of "the might have been" which he had once felt during his intercourse with Sabine. Then, later, she occupies a larger place in his heart through his ardent friendship for her brother Olivier.

To the history of this brother and sister M. Rolland devotes a whole volume of the novel. Here, with many an autobiographical touch, he paints the youth of Antoinette and Olivier in a little provincial French town, which has much in common with his native Clamecy; he brings them to Paris; tells of Olivier training for the teaching profession, of his sister's devotion, of their travels together in Switzerland, and of Antoinette's death just as she had led her brother to the threshold of success. Olivier, some one has said, is M. Rolland as he is, while Christophe is M. Rolland as he would like to be. The brotherly and sisterly affection which unites Antoinette and Olivier, if one may hazard a guess, is an echo of the writer's own experience.

M. Rolland presents us with two Frances, the false France and the true. The characters of Antoinette and Olivier represent the true France, the France we are to meet again in *Dans la Maison*. In the fifth volume, *La Foire sur la Place*, M. Rolland paints the false France. In earlier volumes he had depicted the false and the true Germany, distinguishing between her maudlin sentimentality and her robust, noble idealism. Now in no less vivid colours he paints the false France, the hypocritical cosmopolitan France, the only France, alas! with which Europeans casually visiting Paris ever become acquainted, the France which the expression "French novel" or "French play" generally conjures up before the average British mind. This France, in her various manifestations, in her literature, her drama, her music, and in her purely social aspect, M. Rolland does not hesitate to condemn, and in terms almost as denunciatory as those of the Hebrew prophets whom he admires. From this France, so different from the noble, the free France for which he had pined amidst the limitations of his German home, Christophe turns away in disgust.

"It is not possible," he said to his guide, Sylvain Kohn, a Jew he had known in boyhood and met again in Paris, ". . . there must be something else."

"What more would you have?" asked Kohn.

"France," replied Christophe.

"We are France," said Sylvain.

"There is something else," repeated Christophe.

"Well, old chap, then look for it," said Sylvain.[1]

And Christophe did look for that "something else"; he knew it existed, he had seen its clear reflection in the eyes of the little French governess when he sat by her at the

[1] *La Foire sur la Place*, p. 142.

play, when he passed her in the train, when he caught a brief vision of her across the crowded Paris street. But that "something else" was difficult to find, for it was well hidden. A whole year he had lived in Paris, and all the people he had met seemed intent on nothing save self-amusement or the mimicry of those who amused themselves. But a gleam of that "something else" came to him when he chanced to fall ill and to be waited on by Sidonie, a little servant-girl drudge. In Sidonie's aristocratic pride, instinctive honesty, cheerful disinterestedness, and devotion to duty, he began dimly to comprehend the genius of her race. "You haven't seen any French people yet," said Sidonie. "You have only seen rich folk, and they are the same all the world over." Then Christophe began to seek for a Frenchman whom he might love for the love of France; and when he found him, who should this Frenchman be but Olivier, the brother of Antoinette, Christophe's little French governess!

Christophe's friendship with Olivier was the most significant, the most fruitful, the most intense of all his experiences. In almost every life, studied as a whole, there may be discovered some phase, some experience or series of experiences, which seem to be a kind of climax towards which all previous years and from which all succeeding years appear to flow. If this climax be happy, as it was for Christophe, then happy is he for whom it endures to the end. For Christophe it did not thus endure. After a few years of blissful companionship he and Olivier were parted by death.

The history of Christophe has throughout a double meaning—one purely personal, the evolution of a human soul, the other allegorically international—the blending in one temperament of the tendencies of Eastern and Western, of Teutonic and Celtic culture.

In days when the arrogant aggressiveness of pan-Germanism was already alienating Frenchmen it required some courage for a French novelist to choose a German hero. M. Rolland, gifted as we have seen both by descent and experience with a keen insight into racial psychology, did not hesitate to display this boldness. He chose a German hero, so he tells us, in order to show how salutary may be the contact of French and

German spirits. Differing widely, each one is the complement of the other. Christophe's rebellious Teutonic soul from the time of his first coming to France had been moulded and fashioned by the Latin spirit ; by contact with which he had acquired a certain lucidity and delicacy of sentiment foreign to his race and to him hitherto. This formative work is carried on and completed in Christophe by his friend Olivier. And Olivier, in his turn, is transformed by contact with a nature as strong, as turbulent, as broad as the waters of Christophe's great river, the Vater Rhein. If, as Rolland has written, "France is woman," then Germany is man ; and in Christophe's affection for Olivier there is something as strong and protective as the affection of a man for a woman. Christophe had ever found delight in sacrificing himself for those whom he loved. In boyhood when there were not enough potatoes to go round, Christophe, though tortured with hunger, had feigned loss of appetite in order that his little brothers might be fed. Yet Christophe himself does not admit that he has ever *sacrificed* himself. "I did such and such," he said, "because I was compelled to, and because if I had done otherwise I should have been unhappy." It is Christophe's joy to give himself to his friends. This joy he experiences to the full in his relation with Olivier. For the two friends chance to fall in love with the same woman, Jacqueline Langerie. Christophe, on discovering the state of his friend's heart, conceals his love both from Jacqueline and Olivier. He gives up Jacqueline to Olivier, and for a time he gives up Olivier to Jacqueline. But never for a moment does he permit the lovers to see a cloud upon his brow or to catch a sigh in his voice. For Christophe believed that a sacrifice made sadly was not worth the making.[1]

Jacqueline, alas! is unworthy of Christophe's love or of Olivier's. Not that she is incapable of deep affection or of high seriousness, but, an egoist at heart, she is the kind of woman whom prosperity spoils; had she been condemned to work for a living her nobler characteristics might have triumphed; but when wealth and prosperity come to her and to her husband she grows discontented, she wearies Olivier. She has never

[1] *Les Amies*, p. 133.

comprehended "that marriage is a defiance of Nature,[1] and that once one has thrown down the gauntlet before Nature one must expect her to take it up, and one must prepare to fight gallantly the battle one has provoked."

Jacqueline, having deserted Olivier, he came back to Christophe. The reunited friends met every day and found their intercourse even more pleasant and helpful than before. Olivier endeavoured to forget his heart's bitterness in social service. Together he and Christophe faced the great social problems of the day. In describing their adventures in the world of syndicalism and industrialism, M. Rolland employs a pen as caustic and as vivid as that he had used in sketching the professional and fashionable world of Paris. Through his hero M. Rolland discusses such actual problems as the efficacy of the strike and the question of the minimum wage. "Every man," says Christophe, "whether he work or not has a right to the means, the minimum means, of living.

[1] "Nothing in our life is natural, neither celibacy nor marriage, while free love delivers the weak into the power of the strong. The whole of society is unnatural."—*Les Amies*, pp. 268–9.

Every piece of work, whether good or mediocre, should be paid for, not according to its actual worth—who is an infallible judge of that ?—but according to the lawful and normal needs of the worker. To the artist, the scholar, the inventor, who adorns or serves it, society owes a pension sufficient to give him time and means for adorning and serving it further, nothing more. The *Joconda* is not worth a million. It is impossible to establish any relation between a sum of money and a work of art ; the latter is neither above nor below, but distinct from money. It is not a question of paying for it but of giving the artist a means of livelihood."[1]

In this passage, and in many others in the ninth volume of *Jean Christophe, Le Buisson Ardent*, one can trace the influence of the author's master, Tolstoy. It was indeed in the shadow cast over his soul by Tolstoy's death that Rolland wrote this volume. He had just offered to his master's memory that superb tribute, his *Life of Tolstoy*.

In the retirement of a Swiss village Rolland was recovering from a serious illness occa-

[1] *Le Buisson Ardent*, p. 67.

sioned by an accident in the streets of Paris, from which he narrowly escaped with his life. With his left arm broken the solace of his beloved piano was denied him. The iron of grief had entered into his soul. Away from the din of cities, apart from the noise of the multitude, in the contemplation of the tragedy of Tolstoy's troubled life, were borne in upon Rolland all the possibilities of tumult and ruin and disorder latent in human society and in the human soul. Human progress! what is it? What moral progress has there been from the days of Pericles down to those of M. Fallières? Our so-called civilization, what is it but a thin crust concealing and confining for a time the great welter of chaos? The grumblings of the rushing, roaring torrents of this hidden abyss, the passions of the crowd threatening to rend society in one great cataclysm—"the Revolution," as the friends of Christophe and Olivier describe it, this is the subject of the first part of *Le Buisson Ardent*.

Olivier's death in a manifestation of the 1st of May suddenly severs Christophe's connexion with the industrial world. When

Olivier returned to him he had been in a mood of serene and exalted self-confidence. After his friend's death the obscure currents, ever seething in the nether world of man's nature, broke loose and, bearing down the frail rampart of Christophe's self-control, submerged his soul. Once again he fell a victim to the violence of passion. When the whirlwind had passed he was left as one dead. He had no reason for living, yet he lived. He went and came. "Happy those whom the blood[1] of a strong race supports in life's eclipses," wrote Rolland, in a Barrèsien mood. The limbs of his father and grandfather sustained the body of their son who was about to fall. Life came to him again, as to the prophet of old, in the sound of a rushing mighty wind. And Christophe communed with the spirit of life.[2] "I am freewill fighting and striving eternally. Fight and strive with me," said the spirit. "Fight, always fight!" murmurs Christophe. "Yea, you must always fight," replies the spirit. . . . "And the rhythm of the battle is harmony supreme. Yet not for mortal ears is that harmony. Be content to know

[1] *Le Buisson Ardent*, p. 316. [2] *Ibid.*, pp. 324–5.

that it exists. Do your duty in peace and leave the rest to the gods."

The voice of the spirit, like Uncle Gottfried's of old, brought peace and serenity to Christophe's soul. He went forth cheerfully to his daily task. The creative power which had forsaken him returned. His soul was like the lark which he perceived on one of his rambles; the bird was about to soar out of a burning bush, a thicket of autumn glory, and Christophe knew it would descend to earth again, but he knew also that it would reascend, singing to those on earth below its bright song of the joys of heaven above. "When one can make mistakes with impunity, one is sure of succeeding in the end," wrote Renan. "Happy those who collaborate in the great final success, the complete coming of God."

From a purely artistic point of view *Le Buisson Ardent* may not rank so high as the earlier volumes of *Jean Christophe*, but estimated morally, socially, and psychologically, it is unsurpassed by anything Romain Rolland has written.

In the last volume, *La Nouvelle Journée*, we find Christophe like a great lion tamed.

With all his wildness past, he lies in glad serenity and harmlessness at the feet of his Una, the beautiful Grazia, whom he had known and charmed as a little girl. We met her first in *La Foire sur la Place*. Christophe was her music master, whom she loved with a silent girlish adoration. Sundered by time and circumstance from the object of her youthful affection, Grazia, from her place of power as the wife of a famous diplomat, had followed Christophe's career and protected him from afar, he all the while ignoring whence came the mysterious benefits she bestowed. Now in *La Nouvelle Journée* they are united, in what Rolland calls "a mystic platonic marriage." Their love was for Christophe an inexhaustible fount of peace and strength and joy even after Grazia's death. His vehement passions brought to heel and held in leash, life was no longer a perpetual combat. Grazia had marvelled to see such a humble heart in the man she had known so violent and so proud.

Now Christophe, from the high tower of middle age, looks down upon the life of the new generation, of young Italy, of young France. The new aims, the new ideals, the new activities animating and engaging the youth around him make Christophe feel strangely aloof. But "*la zone de la haine desormais passée*,"[1] as he wrote to Grazia, Christophe regards with a certain tolerance these new currents of thought and activity, even such retrogressive movements as the revival of Catholicism, the hatred of naturalism, and the passion for all manner of mysticism and occultism then possessing French youth. The militarist and Catholic reaction he regarded as a storm, which it is useless to resist; all one can do is to await its passing. It seemed to him that human reason was worn out. It had just made a gigantic effort. Sleep now overcame it; and like a child, tired after a long day, it was saying its prayers before falling asleep.[2] "Let it rest," said Christophe, "for to-morrow it will awake refreshed, freer, and more alert."

The new woman, too, in her various phases, interested Christophe. He regarded as one of the most hopeful signs of the times the effort she was making to free herself from "the unhealthy, degrading domesticity to

[1] P. 248. [2] *La Nouvelle Journée*, p. 271.

which man in his stupid egoism had relegated her, to his own misfortune and to hers."

Christophe travelled through Europe. For the first time he visited Rome, and her glory flooded his soul. He revisited Germany and Switzerland.

German readers of *Jean Christophe*, in letters which now ring sadly false, have expressed their gratitude to M. Rolland for his noble endeavour to reconcile the two nations. The author of an open letter addressed to Romain Rolland, which appeared in the *Berliner Tageblatt*, on December 22, 1912, thanked him for his introduction into French fiction of "a German hero who is not merely held up to ridicule, a fate which has hitherto attended every German in French novels." "Your *Jean Christophe*," he continued, "has done more to unite us to Young France than all the leagues, banquets, and diplomatists." That the union, if it ever existed, was short-lived, was not M. Rolland's fault. No one can fail to admire him for this fine attempt to reconcile the two nations.

Great books, to be appreciated, must be read leisurely; and the appearance of the parts of *Jean Christophe* at intervals of a few months in *Les Cahiers de la Quinzaine* enabled readers to savour to the full all its rich vitality. They came to look upon the German musician as an intimate friend. But everything must have an end ; and the rumour was spread abroad that the tenth volume of the novel was to see the end of Jean Christophe. Many were the conjectures of readers as to how their hero was to die. Surely a character drawn on so colossal a scale could have no ordinary end ! In the passing of this great hurricane of a life something apocalyptic was expected. Would Christophe, like Empedocles, in whose philosophy Christophe's creator had often found inspiration, hurl himself from a mountain top into the mouth of a volcano ? But no, such an end would have been out of keeping with a work in which all the great incidents take place in the spiritual realm. Christophe dies quietly in his bed. In his last hours he reviews his life. Then, like a river, he merges in the ocean of eternity.

Turning over the last page of the last volume of *Jean Christophe* is like bidding farewell to an old friend. In the experience of the present writer the close of only one other novel has ever produced a similar effect. That novel was *Les Misérables*. Though differing widely in most respects, these two works, *Jean Christophe* and *Les Misérables*, have one point in common: they are both intensely alive. Once having made the acquaintance of Victor Hugo's Jean Valjean, the hero of *Les Misérables*, of Romain Rolland's Jean Christophe, they enter into one's life, they are never forgotten.

JÉRÔME THARAUD
JEAN THARAUD

THE WORKS OF JEAN AND JERÔME THARAUD

1899. **Le Coltineur Débile.**

1900. **La Lumière**

1902. **La Légende de la Vierge.**
Dingley l'Illustre Ecrivain.

1903. **Contes Magyars.** (Translated by Jérôme Tharaud.)

1904. **Contes de la Vierge.**
Les Moines de L'Athos.
Les Hôbereaux. (In *Les Cahiers de la Quinzaine.*)

1906. **La Ville et les Champs.** (Containing **Les Hôbereaux** and **L'Ami de L'Ordre.**)
Les Frères Ennemis

1907. **Bar Cochebas.**

1911. **La Maîtresse Servante.**

1912. Hommage au Général Charette in *Les Amis d'Edouard* series
La Fête Arabe.
La Tragédie de Ravaillac.

1913. La Bataille de Scutari et d'Albani.

JÉRÔME THARAUD JEAN THARAUD

JÉRÔME THARAUD, 1874
JEAN THARAUD, 1877

We may regard the brothers Jean and Jérôme Tharaud as essentially writers of Young France; for, with the exception of one short story, all their work has appeared in the present century.

These brothers are the Siamese twins of French fiction. Their identity is more completely merged even than that of the Margueritte when they collaborated. All the Tharauds' writings, including letters, are signed by the double initial J. J. or the single one, which is equally unenlightening. Not even a personal acquaintance solves the mystery, for they generally go about together, and inevitably speak of or address one another as *mon frère*. Puzzling vainly how to disentangle Jean from Jérôme one is haunted by the suspicion that neither is Jean and neither Jérôme, that these designations may be mere *noms de plume*. It remains for the pages of Lorenz's useful bibliography to solve the problem ; and there one may read that Jérôme Tharaud was born at St. Julien (Haute Vienne) in 1874, while Jean first saw the light at the same place three years later. It is mere idle curiosity, however, that is thus gratified ; for in a literary sense Jean and Jérôme are so completely one that not a page of their work ever suggests a dual authorship.

To English readers the Tharauds should be especially interesting, because the novel which first made them famous, *Dingley l'Illustre Ecrivain*, has an Englishman for its hero. As a race we are not afraid to see ourselves as others see us, so we shall not flinch before this portrayal of one of our compatriots, even though it be a biting satire of British imperialism. It is the kind of imperialism, heightened by jingoism, which manifested itself in the nineties ; and English readers will have little difficulty in guessing what famous writer sat for the portrait of Dingley.

The Tharauds' novel appeared in 1902, at the close of the South African War, two years before the formation of *l'Entente Cordiale,* at a moment when our relations with France were by no means cordial, at a moment, indeed, when we were unpopular throughout Europe. The sympathies of the Continent were all with the Boers and President Krüger, whom the authors of this book describe as "aged and half-blind, dragging himself from country to country, soliciting the pity of the nations, weeping and smoking in his hotel bedroom." How that war caused us to be hated abroad! Why it is difficult to tell. Even granted that the war was unjust, other nations have waged unjust wars without kindling such fires of hostility in the breasts of non-combatants. Why should our conquest of these Dutch farmers involve us in so much dislike? Possibly because we had long posed as the friends of oppressed nationalities. Whatever their reason, all continentals took Krüger's side. They all detested us, from the idealists who had hitherto looked to England to champion the cause of small nations to the little French boy who, warned when Krüger passed through Paris of the official order against any anti-English demonstration, said that if he must not cry *à bas les Anglais*, at least he would call out *à bas le roast beef*.

No one should read *Dingley* without taking into account the anti-British atmosphere which pervaded Europe at the time of its publication. Proud egoism and pitiless patriotism were then regarded as the Britisher's dominant characteristics. Mrs. Dingley, who is of French descent, warns her husband to beware lest he become "the apostle of a hard egotistical imperialism."

The Tharauds' conception of Dingley and of the type of imperialism he represents may have been suggested by two brilliant essays which appeared in the first year of the century. The essays were by Chevrillon. They occur in a volume entitled *Études Anglaises*, which is dedicated to Mme. Taine. The first is on Rudyard Kipling, the second on the state of English public opinion during the Transvaal War. If allowances be made for certain distortions and exaggerations which resulted from the Anglophobia then raging throughout Europe, this essay on Rudyard Kipling is one of the most perspicacious appreciations of that great writer which has ever been written. It contributed largely to the vogue which Kipling now enjoys in France. Chevrillon pointed out that Kipling must inevitably appeal to Frenchmen because of his marvellous faculty of construction and arrangement—" Dans la phrase, le paragraphe, la nouvelle, il enfonce, il burine le trait ; il lie et serre avec décision le ligne de contour. . . . Il est court, fort, dense, acèré, comme Mérimèe, bien plus nerveuse, instantané et cruel."

There are situations in *Dingley* which have unmistakably been suggested by passages in Chevrillon's Essay. Thus, for example, Chevrillon's description of Rudyard Kipling's flat on the Thames Embankment, which " looked out on a landscape lost in mist, a dull infinity of brick and the livid river bearing its traffic between cyclopean railway bridges," suggests to the novelists' imagination the following poetic picture: " The fifth storey of an immense block which dominated the life of the Thames. There, when the fog veiled the river, the houses and the quay, he might imagine himself in a lighthouse. His ardent soul plunged into the past. He saw the Vikings on their dragon ships coming up the Thames ; and the noise of the sirens evoked the trumpet-calls of those old sea-kings. Celts, Saxons, Normans, ascended the river. Each brought his own secret ; these a sense of the mystery in things, those a love of adventure. All these peoples mingled in the fog, birds of tempest crying in the northern wind."

There is a passage which Chevrillon quotes from the *Times* newspaper, describing Kipling's departure on board the *Teutonic* for the United States. This paragraph the Tharauds glorify into Dingley's triumphant embarkation for South Africa at Southampton.

Accompanied by his wife and little son, Dingley goes to the war. He goes *en connoisseur* in order to observe certain phases of life and of death. He carries in his notebook the scheme of a new novel, wherein he tells the story of one Barr, a London loafer. Dingley, as he sat in a public-house near Trafalgar Square, had observed Barr stupefied with gin and caught in the recruiting-sergeant's toils. Barr was a good-for-nothing, a creature barely man, more like a lanky, anæmic girl, a colourless wretch sunk in the depths of poverty, down at the heels and down at the mouth. But in the service of the "Widow at Windsor" this piteous being is to be transmogrified into a hero. In London he would have sunk lower and lower, to the dregs of humanity. Once engaged in foreign service, by "the very virtue of war," he will rise to be a man and then to be a hero. With all his heart and soul Dingley believes in the virtue of war. But Mrs. Dingley, who, we remember, is a lady of French extraction, is weak in this faith. When her husband tells her Barr's story, she wonders whether even "the virtue of war" be capable of transforming into a hero a man who enlisted when he was drunk. "Do you think," she asks, "that it is possible for the slaying of men, the pillaging of farms, the violation of women to reform Barr? War may convert into heroes those who are made of heroic stuff, but the others become mere brutes."

"Those are clergymen's or Frenchmen's ideas," exclaims Dingley. "In my opinion a man becomes great in proportion to the greatness of the task in which he engages. My loafers can never become gentlemen; but on what you call their 'brutish instincts' the Empire is built."

In Barr, Dingley intends to personify patience, initiative, self-control, humanitarianism, English good-humour—in a word, English greatness. And by Barr's history he intends to explain the greatness of Cromwell's Ironsides, of Wellington's army, and of the Tommies who guard our dominions in India and in Africa.

In addition to his enthusiastic optimism Dingley is endowed with that peculiarly British cocksureness which, while creating, extending and maintaining the British Empire, has never failed to exasperate foreigners. Never for a moment does Dingley doubt the righteousness of the British cause in South Africa. Yet, though his patriotism be blind and narrow, though it lead him to ignore Napoleon and to worship Disraeli and Cecil Rhodes, though it be ludicrously self-satisfied, surely after all it is not utterly despicable. Without Dingley's kind of patriotism nations would long ago have ceased to exist, or rather they would never have existed at all. And without nations could never have been conceived that international ideal for which we are now fighting.

But are the authors of *Dingley* internationalists? We doubt it. There are passages in their books which seem to prove that they, like Dingley, believe in conquest and in colonization, only that conquest and that colonization must be the work of Frenchmen, and Frenchmen of the old-fashioned kind—moderns, they hold, are just as prone as Dingley to self-satisfaction and cocksureness.

The Tharauds are far from sharing the pacificism of their friend Romain Rolland, to whom this book is dedicated and who was their master at l'École Normale.

But, after all, it is not to them that we must go for any definite theory of life. They are pure artists. They paint beautiful pictures—light, graceful, and delicate, like Corot landscapes, or glowing with the savagery of primitive things, with "nature red in tooth and claw." They love to depict the conditions of primitive culture. They, like their friend Barrès, are possessed by a deep reverence for the past.

Affection for the past and for the glamour of its archaic glory is the note of their novel *La Fête Arabe*. The book tells of the rise, decline, and fall of an African town in the oasis, Ben Nezouh, which is on the verge of French Algeria. The beauty of the East in its primitive natural picturesqueness, its hideousness when corrupted by colonists who are not of the right sort, who are not *vieux Français de France*, this is the theme of *La Fête Arabe*. The hero of the book is one of these old Frenchmen of France, a French army surgeon, who, with an adaptability which is characteristic of his race, has thrown in his lot with the Arabs of Ben Nezouh. While remaining *un vieux Français de France*, he has none the less assimilated that curious blend of culture and barbarity which characterizes the Arabs around him. They call him their Caliph; they have made him their mayor. In the eyes of Ben Nezouh he is a veritable demi-god.

And all goes well until the railway comes to Ben Nezouh. The railway inspires the Caliph with all manner of dreams for his beloved oasis. By advertisement he attracts thither a few *vieux Français de France*. But with these elect rush in multitudes of undesirables—vulgar Mediterranean people—Spaniards, Maltese, Italians, who come to construct the railway, or who follow in its track and ultimately settle in Ben Nezouh. This garden of the African desert they transform into a place as hideous as any suburb of Naples or Palermo. With these decadent Mediterraneans the Caliph wages bitter war. In the end he is defeated. His very Arabian mistress, for whose sake he had lingered too long on the scene of his vanished hopes, betrays him and plots his assassination. Narrowly escaping with his life, he turns his back on Ben Nezouh, with its now absurdly distorted name of *Ben Nezouh Boileau.* He flees from that agonizing picture of Eastern splendour besmirched with Western vulgarity. He penetrates deep into the desert and leads a roaming life with Arabs not yet defiled by contact with the dregs of our so-called civilization.

It is difficult to imagine any subject more fitted to the talent of our authors than that of *La Fête Arabe.* Here the Tharauds take place among that line of French writers who from Montesquieu to Loti have heard the East a' calling, and responded to her summons with all their heart and soul. How completely the authors of *La Fête Arabe* have caught the spirit of the East appears in every page of this fascinating book. Here, for example, they paint the romantic charm of the desert :

"Et puis, pendant cinq jours, ce fut le Haut Plateau, la steppe interminable où l'esprit n'a pour se distraire et rêver que les jeux de la lumière sur des cimes lointaines, le bordj où l'on s'arrête pour changer l'attelage, quelque tentes noires au ras du sol, la caravane qui chemine avec des chameaux goudronnés, ses ânes miniscules et ses petits chevaux. Et toujours, l'obsédante idée que, s'il y à mille ans on était passé lâ, rien n'eut été changé à ce pays de rochers et de cendre, ni à cette vie primitive que je traverse sans bruit."

Even over the homeliest domestic scenes the poetry of the East casts a glamour of romance. On the terrace floor of the Caliph's house was a round hole encircled by a railing. Through this opening one could look down into the gloom of the apartment beneath. "Growing used to the darkness, the eye gradually discerned a fairy-like vision. Round and about the pillars supporting the roof moved silently veils and diadems of gold. In this darkness made visible Oriental splendours gleamed mysteriously.

The faces were unveiled. Perceiving me, one of the women uttered a cry of horror and fled through the pillars. Another, crooning to her child at the breast, paused in her song. Two others, crouching on the ground, persistently leaned over little earthen stoves, which gleamed in the shadow like wondrous gems. Now and again they looked, and, like a lightning flash, I caught the expression of a glance. It was a kitchen. These jewelled women were preparing the evening meal. A vision of one of our drawing-rooms at home came into my mind, and I realized how utterly our civilization has failed in beauty."

Over another of the Tharaud's books, *La Bataille de Scutari et d'Albani*, the glamour of the Orient sheds a charm; but here there enters into the romance something deeper and stronger—all the passions, the virtues and the vices; which are let loose by war.

Jérôme Tharaud, on leaving l'École Normale, had for a time filled the post of *lecteur de l'Université* in one of *ces tristes capitaux des régions du Moyen Danube*. And, as the result of this experience, he, in collaboration with his brother, had written a very striking story, *Bar Cochebas*, which, like most of our authors' early work, made its first appearance in *Les Cahiers de la Quinzaine.*[1] Bar Cochebas was a young Jew, one of Tharaud's pupils at the University; and in a few brief pages the professor has drawn a masterly portrait of his pupil, the son of a drunken village publican, loaded with erudition, yet yearning so passionately for Western culture that he would readily part with all his learning in return for the knowledge of how to hold a fork. We see this scholarly barbarian, returning from the University to his country home, sitting at his desk and hearing in the room below his worthless old father abused and insulted by his customers. "However low he may have fallen," writes Cochebas to his French friend, "can I go on allowing him to be thus insulted? Here on my table lies a revolver, the instrument you have invented for the solution of affairs of honour. . . . As I hear blows and insults falling on my father in the room below, I say to myself, 'fire! fire!' And then I sit quietly at my table, for I know that vengeance would be vain. . . . What effect would my revolver have in this vast plain and in the long succes-

[1] Eighth Series, No. 11.

sion of time ? No more effect than a child's pop-gun."

Yet how vain is this philosophizing, he reflects. It is the enemy of all action. Ideas exercise a terrible power over this young Jew. He has been reading "the Cid." He admires Rodrigo and wishes to emulate him. What is he to do ? he asks his French friend.

"Cease admiring 'the Cid,'" comes the reply. "Far from being what you consider him, the symbol of French honour, he was only a brutal young Spaniard." "Leave all those peasants of the plain," writes his French professor, "I know something about them. They are kind, sympathetic drunkards. And as for Monsieur; your father, why disturb by any useless and dangerous diversion a situation in which he seems so happy ?"

But the advice comes too late : the revolver has been grasped, Cochebas has descended to avenge his father. Then, in the act of firing, impressed suddenly by the vanity of the deed, the philosopher has turned the weapon against himself and ended his wonderings for ever.

When the Balkan War broke out Jérôme Tharaud was seized by a desire to observe his peasants of the plain in the act of fighting. It was an indiscreet curiosity, he frankly confesses, and more than once in the book, *La Bataille de Scutari et d'Albani*, we find him disliking himself for having yielded to it.

But, after all, it is not so much war as the asides of war which are described in these pages. And here we find our authors, with profound insight and sympathy, painting the primitive nature of the Montenegrin people—for it is in Montenegro that Tharaud chiefly makes his observations.

Over all these descriptions the note which dominates is the persistence, even in this twentieth century, of primitive conditions. Progress, according to these writers, that malevolent spirit, that vague, formless, faceless thing, seldom enters here. In Montenegro the conditions of life are still almost Homeric. Though the aged King Nicholas appears in his motor-car, driven by his daughter, Princess Xenia, there is something about him which reminds one that in the conflicts between pastoral tribes, "beneath the same skies, over these same plains, kings' daughters drove chariots behind swift coursers." For the

Montenegrins, though they condescend to the modernity of taking a train, the moment arrives when they resort to a more primitive form of travel. The train stops, the passengers, including the King and the Princess, descend and form themselves into a procession to go on foot and join the train which, disburdened; continues its climb, on the opposite side of the mountain. "Quel agreste cortège," write the Tharauds, "sur ce haut sommet désolé ! Ce vieux roi suivi de ces femmes, c'est un roi de fable ou de légende, Ulysse ou le vieux Lear au bras de Cordélia !" The King's cap, starred with gold, his red waistcoat metal buttoned, his light green coat, his blue breeches and high boots, his revolver hanging from his portly waist, give him the air of some mountaineer from Tchema Gora.

What a procession ! And it is only one of many, all equally striking, which move through the pages of this fascinating book.

"That which I see passing before me," writes the author, "is eternal war, the war of ancient Egypt, of Assur, and of Nineveh ; the campaigns of the Gauls, the ravages of the Huns, the hordes of the Thirty Years

War, Turenne in the Palatinate, the Cossacks in l'Ile de France, the Prussians on the Loire; war that nothing can change, war of yesterday, war of to-morrow."

Not so eternal as war, yet centuries old and comparatively untouched by time, are the religions of these people: Islam, who in the muezzin's evening prayer seems to cry: "I am rest, repose, contemplation, humility, wisdom"; and the Christian Church, entrenched for ten centuries on her Holy Hill, in the superb isolation of Mount Athos. Thence she dominates Eastern Christendom, yet for five hundred years she has groaned in the thraldom of the Turk. In the eyes of a Greek pilgrim who, in perfect security and heedlessness, had wandered through the Balkans, unhurt by fleeing Turks or Macedonian war-bands or Albanian guerillas, all the fighting and the suffering in the Balkan Peninsula had but one object—to free from the oppressor the monks of Mount Athos. For this pilgrim the battlefield was not in the valleys of Montenegro, or on the plains of Thessaly, or in the villages of Albania; it was in Heaven, where the prayers of the monks were besieging the throne of God.

The answer to those prayers, that blessed deliverance so long expected, it was given to the author of this book to witness.

Tharaud had fled from the scene of suffering in Montenegro. "Que fais—je ici à regarder si complaisamment la douleur," he had asked.

It is degrading, he feels, idly to watch men suffer; and, determined to flee from hospital sights, his mind turns to his pilgrim's holy mountain and to his "castles of the soul."

Some years before, Tharaud had visited Mount Athos; and, in collaboration with M. Henri Lebeaud, he had contributed a description of it to *Les Cahiers*. The pages in his later book which depict these fortified mountains, inhabited by a vast army of praying monks, whose contemplations Gibbon has so eloquently described, are some of the most artistic and the most poetical the Tharauds have ever written.

Among much in the habits of this community that is absolutely unique, one feature is especially singular: it is the curious contradiction of the misogamy of these ten thousand monks all ranged beneath the banner of a woman, yet banishing from their midst, not woman only, but every female creature. "Sur le Mont Athos," writes Tharaud, "tout vit pour cette vierge sombre." But the Mediterranean and the Southern Seas which adjoin it seem to possess a wonderful power of casting into an enchanted slumber those who have lingered on her shores. "Tout vit on plutôt tout s'endort," continues Tharaud, "tout est déjà endormi. Cette religion orthodoxe a un prodigieux appétit de la mort et du sommeil."

It is not always in foreign lands, in Greece, in Montenegro, or in Africa, that the Tharauds seek these primitive conditions, these survivals of the *Le bel Autrefois*, which they adore. They find them close at home, in their natal province, in the romantic, legend-loving Limousin. Like true *Barrèsiens*, though electing to live in Paris, the Tharauds profess a passion for country life. They love to catch the echoes of their dear former time ringing through the woods and valleys of rural France; and the mystery, the pathos, and the touching seriousness of country-folk they have expressed with power and charm in two of their novels, *Les Hôbereaux* and *La Maîtresse Servante*.

It is by the last of these two books that the Tharauds, when familiar to any English readers, are generally known in England. But *Les Hôbereaux*, though possessing less unity of design, is almost as masterly a study as *La Maîtresse Servante* of a certain phase in French provincial life. In both these stories and in another, *L'Ami de L'Ordre*, which is contained in the same volume as *Les Hôbereaux*, our authors constantly contrast life in Paris with life in the country—and always to the disadvantage of the former. " Paris," cry these dwellers in the capital, " est la ville des sansfoyers, qui n'ont ni une maison ni une terre à défendre . . . la ville des fous . . . des ambitieux . . . Paris est la tête pourrie d'une France saine."

It is in the country that these writers discover that stability and conservatism which they admire, and those *existences tourmentées* into which, with consummate art, they weave a thread of romance.

The same world and the same class of society they depict alike in *Les Hôbereaux* and *La Maîtresse Servante*. *Hôbereau* is the term applied to a country gentleman, something between an English squire and an English yeoman farmer. The class is rapidly dying out in England; and in France, we fancy, it lingers only in a few remote regions of the countryside. To this class belongs the hero of *La Maîtresse Servante*. In a charming booklet on this novel,[1] M. Barrès, the inspirer of so much of the Tharauds' work, describes the hero of this novel as one of those wild creatures with a nature at once tamed and corrupted by society. Sent to study in Paris, he becomes unclassed and isolated in the life of the capital. Then, compelled to return to his country home and to lead the life of his ancestors, he throws conventions to the winds and openly instals his mistress in a house near the château where he lives with his mother. The mother imagines that the only way to estrange the mistress from her lover is to humiliate her: she employs her therefore in the château as a seamstress, little by little degrading her to the rank of a servant; and to this humiliation the mistress, who is miserable in the

[1] Published in *Les Amis d'Edouard* series. These beautiful booklets are privately printed by M. Edouard Champion for his friends. It is to the kindness of "Edouard's" brother, M. Pierre Champion, that I am indebted for a sight of this graceful and discerning essay.

isolation and inactivity of her life, submits and finally resigns herself.

"This novel," writes Barrès, "presents the portrait of a mind and heart contracting and hardening in contact with life. Because the hero fails to realize his heart's aspirations and to encourage the development of his powers he remains sunk in mediocrity." The most lovable character in the book is *La Maîtresse*, but even she sometimes repels through excessive meekness. The hero's mother is of a type with which, alas! we are all well acquainted. *Elle se faisait une certaine idée chagrine de la vie.* She flees from happiness and runs to meet trouble. With such an unattractive and apparently commonplace trio as the chief characters of their story, it is marvellous how our novelists contrive to construct a romance which is at once gracefully poetical and deeply significant, a novel which Barrès has described as *un sombre petit chef d'œuvre.*

Such keen observers of primitive human nature as the Tharauds cannot fail to be attracted by religious emotion. In their attitude towards the Church the Tharauds resemble their master, Barrès: mentally they are agnostics, emotionally they are Catholics. As Frenchmen and traditionists they cannot fail to sympathize with Catholicism. At the same time they agree with Emerson that all religions are the same wine in different coloured glasses. They are struck by the profound resemblance between the Faith of the Cross and the Faith of the Crescent. "Cette religion grecque et l'Islam," they write, "expriment l'une et l'autre les mêmes conceptions orientales, le même abandon au destin, la même contemplation assoupie."

In *Les Frères Ennemis*, a story of the reformation at Geneva, and in their tales of the Virgin, old legends retold with the charm of the mediæval *conteurs*, the subject is religious. But a much more profound treatment of the religious emotion may be found in a later work, the *Tragédie de Ravaillac*, the story of Henry IV's murderer. Out of musty, dead, old parchments, out of Ravaillac's depositions at his trial and entries in the registers of his native Angoulême, the Tharauds, with their own peculiar art, have fashioned a vivid, a pathetic, and a deeply significant narrative.

Ravaillac was one of those souls in which the religious sentiment, growing into fanaticism, verges on madness. Obsessed by a single idea or series of ideas, such devoted souls from Joan of Arc, through the line of Ignatius Loyola, John Bunyan, Charles Wesley, down to Charlotte Corday, have moulded the destinies of mankind. Ravaillac might have been one of these had he been but slightly different. But his father was a drunkard, and with his religious zeal were blended weakness of will and feebleness of intellect. Ravaillac's history is the perpetual conflict between ardour and irresolution. For months the desire to slay the King, the pseudo-Catholic, the protector of Huguenots, the ally of Huguenot princes, possessed his poor soul and vainly strove to express itself in action.

Twice he tramped all the way from Angoulême to urge Henry to make war on the Huguenots. Twice he returned to Angoulême, having done nothing save cry vainly to the King as he passed on the highway for permission to speak with him. Meanwhile, taking shape in his feeble mind, was the idea that his poor arm must be the avenging arm of the Lord. The idea again impels him to trudge the long road from Angoulême to Paris, wondering all the while whether the idea may not be a sin, hesitating to receive the Holy Sacrament, kneeling behind his mother as she receives it in the hope that a crumb of the Divine grace, which enters into her, may find its way into his own distracted soul. At Paris, this third time, the would-be assassin, who had hitherto gone unarmed, sees a knife lying by his side on the inn table. For Ravaillac this knife is what the revolver had been for Cochebas. Like the Danubian Jew, he conquers his vacillation and seizes it ; and the possession of that knife gives some stability to his poor flickering will. Yet again he quits Paris with his purpose still unachieved ; but the knife is with him ; he feels it pressing against his cuirass, and for a moment he longs to return, but the glory of a spring day surrounds him, life smiles on him, and he fears the darkness of death which for him as well as for his victim must follow the doing of this deed. He longs for a sign from Heaven. If only he could throw away the knife, but he cannot bring himself to part with it, and instead he sharpens it on a stone by the wayside. Night falls, and through the darkness looms a calvary. The poor harassed pilgrim throws himself on his knees before the image of Christ. Then he rises and takes the road to Paris—never to return. This time the deed is done.

Here again the Tharauds have realized that ambition to which they aspired in *La Maîtresse Servante*. They have shown themselves the poets of *une existence tourmenté*. And all the more striking is Ravaillac's sad, morose personality when it is contrasted with that of his gay, pleasure-loving victim, the light-hearted King, who is absorbed in his last intrigue, the vain endeavour to win the love of a beautiful princess.

Somewhat out of place appears the last chapter of this book, the story of Carnot's murderer. The parallel is not very close between the perpetually-hesitating Ravaillac and the resolute baker's boy, who, once he has conceived it, moves swiftly to the accomplishment of his purpose.

None of the Tharauds' novels abound in incident. Their plots move indolently. "Les Tharaud savent patienter," writes Barrès, "s'il le faut, ils attendent dix années dix lignes qui achèvent de donner au chapitre son caractère véridique et au livre sa perfection." It is seldom that the wealth or rapidity of the action distracts the reader from the artistic form, the poetry of the narrative. Yet now and again these simple souls, whom the Tharauds love to portray, are convulsed by brutal passions surging up from the depths of their subconsciousness, survivals of a long-forgotten primitive past when man was much nearer than now to the level of the dumb creation. Then, gushing forth from the authors' imagination, with all the rapidity of a mountain torrent incident follows incident. Thus it is in *L'Ami de l'Ordre*, when the idealist Communard, who knows that his fatal hour has struck, is seized by the wild fury of desire for the watchmaker's wife who stands before him; thus again in *Les Hôbereaux*, when the peasants of Périgord, during the war of 1870, set upon and do to death, with all the barbarity of the dark ages, a country squire who has dared to suggest that the Prussian fire-arms are better than the French.

Such incidents even before the War helped one to realize how near to the surface, in

Oostvleteren 19 janvier 1915

Cher Edouard, quelle merveille ce saucisson! Et le chocolat de Debauve et Gallais! Pour dire leur excellence il faudrait Brillat Savarin! Merci aussi du Montaigne. Il nous aide à passer bien des heures de brume et d'ennui. C'est une lecture qui convient parfaitement à des quartiers d'hiver, près d'un poêle. Le jour où il nous arriva, nous lûmes dans l'après midi l'exhortation à la mort. Le soir, il nous passa au dessus de la tête trente marmites de première grandeur. Les pieds dans la boue, nous vîmes passer avec tranquillité ces constellations bizarres, en nous remémorant in petto les conseils de l'excellent Judéo-Bordelais.
Ça sert la philosophie! Pour une fois... sais-tu...

Présente nos meilleurs souvenirs, je te prie, à ta famille.

Tes amis
J. J. Tharaud.

AUTOGRAPH LETTER WRITTEN BY M. THARAUD AT THE FRONT TO M. EDOUARD CHAMPION AT PARIS
Reproduced by M. Champion's kind permission

spite of our so-called modern progress, are the passions of *l'autrefois*, the brutality of the past. Now, having lost none of their cruel barbarity, these primitive impulses well up to the surface once more. And, at present much more closely than ever in the Balkan War, is it given to the Tharauds to observe them. For they, with many another young writer of France, exchanging the pen for the sword, now serve their country at the front. From the trenches they have written to their friend, M. Edouard Champion, the letter, which he has kindly permitted to be reproduced in facsimile on the opposite page. Acknowledging a volume of Montaigne's *Essays*, they write, " How many hours of fog and boredom does it not beguile! What book could be more welcome to those who sit round the stove in winter quarters! On the afternoon of the day it arrived, we read the exhortation to death. In the evening there whizzed over our heads thirty 'Jack Johnsons' of the biggest. With our feet in the mud, we contemplated with tranquillity those chequered constellations, thinking on the counsels of that excellent Bordelasian Jew. There's philosophy for you!"

RENÉ BOYLESVE

THE WORKS OF RENÉ BOYLESVE

1896. **Le Médecin des Dames de Néans.**
Les Bains de Bade.
1897. **Sainte Marie des Fleurs.**
1899. **Mademoiselle Cloque.**
Le Parfum des Iles Borromées.
1901. **La Becquée.**
1902. **La Leçon d'Amour dans un Parc.**
1903. **L'Enfant à la Balustrade.**
1905. **Le Bel Avenir.**
1908. **Mon Amour.**
1911. **Le Meilleur Ami.**
1912. **La Jeune Fille bien Elevée.**
1912. **Madeleine Jeune Femme.**
1913. **La Marchande de Petits Pains pour les Canards.**

RENÉ BOYLESRE

RENÉ BOYLESVE, 1867

To M. René Boylesve more than to any other writer discussed in this book belongs the title of novelist. For fiction in the strictest sense of the term is every one of his fourteen volumes. They place him in the front rank of European writers on the eve of the War.

His first novel, *Le Médecin des Dames de Néans*, appeared in 1896. Since then he has contributed to French fiction twelve more novels, and one collection of short stories, *La Marchande de Petits Pains pour les Canards*. In subtlety of treatment, in profound psychology, and in artistry of design these works present an equality hardly to be found in any other French novelist of to-day. Not that all M. Boylesve's novels are of equal merit. This would not be true of him or of any other writer worth considera-tion. Indeed, in comparison with some of his most aspiring works, such as *La Becquée*, *L'Enfant à la Balustrade*, *Mademoiselle Cloque*, or *Madeleine Jeune Femme*, others, *Mon Amour*, or *Le Meilleur Ami*, for example, are mere sketches. Nevertheless every one of M. Boylesve's works may without exaggeration be pronounced such a piece of fine and finished literary workmanship as could only be produced by one who is a master of his art.

In M. Boylesve's work, as in M. Rolland's, it is not difficult to discern a certain racial influence. But Boylesve, unlike the author of *Jean Christophe*, is essentially French. He hails from that fountain of pure French, Touraine, the ancient garden of France. And over all his work the serene atmosphere of that Loire country, the limpid clearness of its rivers, the subtle irony united to what has been called *le bon sens libre et railleur*, of those who dwell upon their banks, shed a vague but irresistible charm.

The land of the Loire in M. Boylesve's novels plays a part not unlike the regions of the Meuse in the novels of M. Barrès. Yet both these writers live chiefly in Paris. Paris, however, has not deracinated them as it did Sturel and his companions in M. Barrès' famous novel. Boylesve, like Barrès, keeps heart and mind in tune with the spirit of the countryside which gave him birth.

Not a bad touchstone of a man's nature is his attitude towards the corner of the world in which he first saw the light. When you find a man returning to his native village and seeing there nothing but pettiness and vanished illusion and alienated sympathy, when you see him hugging himself with delight as he turns his back on boorish rustics and his face towards the polite metropolis, then may you not conclude that in this man's heart lurks no tenderness for the past, that his sympathies are entirely with the future, and will you be mistaken if you surmise that in philosophy he is an aggressive Rationalist and in politics a pronounced Radical and Socialist?

If you find a man, on the other hand, moved to tears, stirred to the depths of his being by the sight of the landscape that cradled him, by some familiar tree, by some village steeple or some cottage door, surely you may infer that in this man's temperament, deep down perhaps and hidden in his subconsciousness, there runs a current of conservatism, keeping him in touch with the past. That man, if only in some remote corner of his being, is celebrating the rites of *le culte des morts*.

"The spirit of the *boulevardier des boule-*

vards," writes Lemaître, who, like Boylesve, was a Touranian,[1] "does not carry one far. Every one should have a village steeple. When I return to the country and, from the carriage which has fetched me from the station, discern my village belfry appearing on the horizon, my soul is stirred. I seem to be returning to a healthier, truer life, and in this haven for good hearts and simple I can judge in a clearer light the artificial world which I have just quitted."

One remembers how Charles Lamb's heart was stirred within him when he and his cousin Bridget revisited Mackery End, where they had passed some of childhood's happiest hours. To these faithful souls the charm of reality seemed to surpass even their youthful recollections. "Still the air," writes Lamb, "breathed balmily about it; the season was in the 'heart of June,' and I could say with the poet:

> But thou, that didst appear so fair
> To fond imagination,
> Dost rival in the light of day
> Her delicate creation.[2]

[1] *Contemporains*, vol. v, pp. 262–3.
[2] "Mackery End, in Hertfordshire." *Essays of Elia*.

M. Boylesve, like Lamb and Lemaître, has a deep affection for the past. His heart was thrilled when, after years of absence, he returned to the country of his birth. He was moved to the centre of his being as he made his way through the narrow streets of the little town, where he was born and bred, to the garden railing, dominating the high street, where as a boy he used to lean and watch the comings and goings of the townsfolk. With a melancholy joy he tramped as of yore over the stubble fields of Courance, the family domain, where he had often dwelt in childhood. With reverend piety his due feet did not fail to tread the cemetery's hallowed ground, wherein were laid the three women to whom he owed his life: the graves, he writes, "of her who gave it me, of her who by her tender care kept it for me, of her, my great-aunt Félicie, to whom in youth I was indebted for a small fortune."[1]

To this and subsequent visits paid by M. Boylesve to the Loire country we owe the novels which contain his best work: *Mademoiselle Cloque*, *La Becquée*, *L'Enfant à la Balustrade*, and *La Jeune Fille bien Elevée*.

[1] *Mon Amour*, pp. 142 *et passim*.

The link between these books and his Touraine sojournings he has himself described in his preface to *La Becquée*.

One day, he writes, "I returned to the country of my childhood, where my parents died and where they were born. I unlocked the garden gate and the house door; I opened cupboards, I walked along the corridor, and in my memory the deserted house was filled with inhabitants and with life. I was so moved by all I saw that, even long after my return to Paris, where one forgets everything, the impression left by my visit persisted and seemed to dominate all my other memories. It was, I think, because this impression was made by something far and away beyond my personal emotions, because the scenes and the faces which my natal air evoked were scenes and faces common to the French provincial family from which have sprung so many men who to-day are in their thirties."

It is this French provincial family that M. Boylesve has powerfully portrayed in his four novels of Touraine and in certain stories of his last volume, *La Marchande de Petits Pains pour les Canards*.

One would grossly misjudge M. Boylesve if on closing these novels of Touraine one were to assume a knowledge of our author's work. For his versatility and fertility of imagination are no less remarkable than his command of literary art.

To form any accurate opinion of his work it is necessary to read every novel he has written. A study of only one or two gives a very false impression of his genius. One might read *Mademoiselle Cloque* and *La Jeune Fille bien Elevée* and think: here is a writer whose minute and vivid picture of simple provincial life, portrayed with a reserve of expression and imagination which are rare in French fiction, might with impunity be put into the hands of any *jeune fille*, however *bien elevée* in M. Boylesve's sense of the term. Then one turns to such novels as *Le Parfum des Îles Borromées* or *Le Bel Avenir*, and one is startled to find how widely erroneous was such a judgment. Here are novels the frank voluptuousness or the candid realism of which might, to use the librarian's phrase, "unfit them for general circulation." But on reading *Sainte Marie des Fleurs*, *Mon Amour*, and *Madeleine Jeune Femme*, again one is disconcerted. For here though the delicate problem of sex relations be treated, it is with a reserve entirely absent from those other works we have just mentioned.

This astounding versatility constitutes one of M. Boylesve's most powerful attractions. There is no sameness in his novels. He is a writer who can take up any theme, who can strike any note in the whole scale of human vicissitude and human emotion in every possible manner, producing from it every possible sound from the soft, barely audible whisper to the loud resonance echoing like a peal of Rabelaisian laughter.

Yet there is unity in M. Boylesve's work, a unity arising as we shall see from his interpretation of life. Human existence in all its vicissitudes, sad and joyous, is M. Boylesve's subject. He is in love with life, and he depicts it with the minuteness of a scientist, the charm of a poet, and the faithfulness of a historian. M. Boylesve's work possesses the detail of the photographic method now so much in vogue. Yet, unlike many modern writers who adopt that method, M. Boylesve is a true artist. Never does he permit the minuteness of the detail to mar the unity of the design. Never does he relapse into those long digressions which impede the progress of many a modern novel. In conception and in execution his novels are artistic.

With the problem novel M. Boylesve will have nothing to do. His reasons for condemning it he has set forth in his interesting preface to *Madeleine Jeune Femme*. In a previous novel, *La Jeune Fille bien Elevée*, of which this is the sequel, he had been accused of treating the problem of girls' education. There were those who attacked him for his advocacy of old-fashioned methods, others for his sympathy with new-fangled ideas. Such an illuminating exposition of his own views of the novelist's art and such a severe indictment of the problem novel as are contained in M. Boylesve's reply to his critics demand its quotation here.

"That which I described," he writes, "was simply a young girl's state of mind at a given period and nothing more. . . . Had I been a moralist or a sociologist I should have taken a side, I should have inclined towards the past or towards what is believed to be the future. But, as a novelist, I am merely on the side of human nature. It is complex, obscure sometimes . . . but it is of itself stronger and richer than it appears in any poor artificial light we can shed upon it when we try too often in mere laziness to arrange, to label, and to classify it.

"It is not we novelists who in our studies determine that a certain character shall appear thus or thus. But it is the character itself which responds to our evocation, to our curiosity, to our efforts, and finally rewards us by confessing, those are my various aspects! We are not complete masters . . . either of our characters or of our plot. I believe that when a novelist introduces into his work any personal bias he is narrowing his art and perhaps falsifying it. . . . A novel is a magic mirror. By a marvellous process of reduction and foreshortening it presents a reflection of life which is too vast for most eyes to comprehend. For the novelist to present this picture is enough. It is for the picture to speak."

Yet even M. Boylesve admits that there can be no work which is absolutely impersonal. No mind can avoid casting over its creation some personal tinge, however vague. Hence some definite tendency is discernible in all good work. M. Boylesve describes it as less the result of deliberation than of *l'ordre secret du génie.*

On the authority therefore of the writer himself one may inquire what is the secret order of his own genius. It is not difficult to discern. It consists in a courageous stoicism in facing the grim facts of human existence. But this stoicism is tempered by a sense of irony which our author has described in one of his novels as nature's slight compensation to us for our misfortunes.[1]

What are the grim facts of human existence which stand out most boldly in M. Boylesve's novels ? Pre-eminently perhaps they are these : the triumph of the strong over the weak, of compromise over ideals, of common sense over poetry, the eternal reign of the commonplace.

Among all the characters of men and women who defile before us in M. Boylesve's

[1] "La compensation légère qu'offre la nature à nos infortunes en nous rendant sensibles à l'ironie des évènements et des choses." *L'Enfant à la Balustrade,* p. 246.

pages, none stands out more boldly than that of *tante* Félicie, the heroine of *La Becquée*, introduced incidentally into subsequent novels, *L'Enfant à la Balustrade* and *Mon Amour*. Félicie is a landed proprietress, a type of woman which the dowry system has rendered not uncommon in France. The land hunger possessed her; she had passed her life in adding to and rounding off the family domain of Courance. She was the one successful member of her family, and all the family failures gathered round her like tiny birds not yet able to fly, whose mouths are ever agape for the food that others are to put into them. Félicie is generous and hospitable in her way. The roof of Courance shelters uncles and aunts, brothers and sisters, nephews and nieces, including the little five-year-old boy, Riquet, who is doubtless in many respects the author himself, and who with all the *naïveté* and keenness of childhood observes and describes this patriarchal community.

Félicie was generous and hospitable, as we have said, but she exacted payment for benefits she conferred in the right to dominate her family. She did not always succeed as well as she would like, but when her relatives escaped from the guidance or rejected the counsel of this latter-day Deborah, it was nearly always to their hurt. Félicie's brother-in-law, Casimir, *grand père Fantin*, is a case in point. He is the incorrigible speculator. Having lost two or three fortunes during the second Empire, wellnigh penniless, he had sought refuge beneath Félicie's roof, and, when a small legacy fell to him, again he speculated, involving his son's little fortune as well as his own. When everything vanished, Casimir, hunted by his creditors, again has recourse to Félicie, who, in disgust, had driven him from her house.

"Mais malheureux! qu'allez-vous manger?" she cries.

"Il se leva, prit le dossier de la chaise de rotin, la balança, en regardant le ciel, et il dit, 'Aux petits des oiseaux il donne la pâture.' . . . Ces dames le contemplaient. À la stupéfaction de leur regard, il se mêlait une sorte de respect pour le don merveilleuse d'insouciance qu'avait reçu cet homme.

"'Enfin,' soupira Félicie, 'il vous reste que le bon homme est taillé pour gagner le centaine, tant qu'il vivra, vous aurez toujours le couvert.' "[1]

Félicie the strong woman, who for her own part had heretofore struggled successfully against the odds of life, was then herself suffering defeat at the hands of a terrible disease. In her youth she had been attractive, not so winsome perhaps as Bathsheba Everdene, her twin in English fiction, but decidedly good to look upon. Now the ravages of cancer appeared in her countenance. And her grand-nephew, in *Mon Amour*, recalls sadly, "sa bouche abîmee par la douleur physique, son teint de cire transparente, sa voix et le grand amour de sa terre, qui'etait visible en toute sa personne."

One by one, with all the grimness and inevitability of the Sophoclean drama, are described in the closing pages of *La Becquée*,

[1] "But, unhappy man, how are you going to live?" He rose, took hold of the back of his rush-bottomed chair, balanced it, and, looking up to the ceiling, said:

"For the young birds He provideth food."

The ladies looked at him in astonishment. But with their amazement was mingled a kind of respect for one so bountifully endowed with equanimity.

"After all," sighed Félicie, "you may console yourself that the good man will live to be a hundred, and as long as he lives, you will always have your bread and cheese."

the steps by which Félicie succumbed to her formidable foe. The land hunger persists to the end, and Félicie on her death-bed endeavours to instil it into the little Riquet whom she has made her heir.

Among the numerous kinsfolk who gathered round her at the last was a pious person of the woman-in-orders type, a Madame Leduc, who used daily to assemble the family in the sick-room for prayers and devotional reading. Félicie patiently endured those lugubrious meditations with their ever reiterated words " death " and *vanitas vanitatum*. But one day, as the others were retiring, Félicie took Riquet by the hand and detained him. Then she said :

" My child, you are too young to understand those strange words. But you have a memory, and later you will recollect what you have heard. Believe your old aunt who is about to appear before the judgment seat of the good God, it isn't true !—everything isn't vain. Their *vanitas vanitatum*, it's the mere chatter of folk who have never been good for anything. Beware of high-sounding words. They are like prematurely ripened fruit, they are tasteless.

"Do you remember when we used to walk out together, how you would lean down and look at the young corn sprouting, then how it would grow big enough for us to see it from the road; how one fine day it was as tall as you were; how another time the wind had swept it as if a flock of sheep had been rolling upon it, and my hair turned grey! and then in the end how we saw it threshed among clouds of dust and counted the number of the bushels! Was that vain? Were we wrong to watch the blades of corn in the fields, to be interested in them and to believe in them as if they were friends? Did they ever deceive us? Did they ever fail to become the bread which Fridolin puts into the oven? Is that bread, which Madame Leduc eats as well as any one else, vanity? And the good wine, with the raspberry aroma, which your Uncle Planté with such pride holds up to the light, blinking the while? And our fir-trees? And the tree-stumps which make such a fine flame in winter? And our sheep? And our good cows? And the beautiful blue cheese on which the peasants live? Mere vanity of course! The fools! why don't they talk about all this in their prayers instead of giving us the creeps with their apocalyptic stories? I, my child, I, thank God for having permitted me to see all these vanities ever being reborn again before my eyes, regularly . . . throughout my tale of sixty-five years.

"Remember this: you must cling fast to something and take hold of it as if there were nothing else in the world. You must fix your eyes on something that is close to you, not on the stars; otherwise you will produce words and not works. Go to bed, my little fellow."

What a fine expression have we here of bold, defiant materialism! How faithfully do these words portray one of the fundamental elements of the French genius, that passionate attachment to the earth and the fruits thereof, and that reverence for the daily toil which maketh it to bring forth and bud that has rendered France one of the most prosperous nations under the sun! The creation of Félicie's character alone would have been sufficient to win for M. Boylesve a high place among novelists.

But there are other characters in the book

which are extremely well drawn. *Grand-père* Fantin we have already described. But what of Félicie's husband? For she had a husband: that Uncle Planté, who admiringly held up the rich red wine. This action was not inexpressive of Uncle's disposition. In his simple rural way he was a voluptuary. After a day's sport he would return home with an uncertain gait. When the hunting season was over he would occupy himself in gardening, or would shut himself into a summer-house where he was said to be sorting seeds. Those who were anxious to stand well with him were kind to Valentine, a farmer's daughter. In the Courance household, Uncle Planté was of little account because his wife preferred to him M. Laballue, an old friend, who was nicknamed Barley Sugar because of his kindly disposition. Uncle Planté was overshadowed by his wife like every one else at Courance. But—and here we have one of those fine shades of human character which M. Boylesve excels in depicting—Planté was sincerely attached to Félicie. Shortly after her death he was found one night lying beneath the fir-trees she had loved. His gun had gone off in his face. Those who understood the mute affection which united this retiring man to his domineering wife were not surprised at the accident.

L'Enfant à la Balustrade is the sequel to *La Becquée;* and here we meet several of the characters who occur in the earlier novel. Again it is Riquet who tells the story, and again he tells it with that naïve pathos, which, as Alfred de Vigny put it, "makes the tears come into one's eyes when a child tells what he has seen."

The tale which Riquet tells is one of the trivial jealousies and rivalries of a small country town, described with the humour of a Barrie and the minuteness of a Balzac or an Arnold Bennett. But through the Dædalian maze of this petty provincial life there runs, like Ariadne's thread, a deeper theme. It is the theme of Wordsworth's "Ode on the Intimations of Immortality." "The glory and the dream" of Riquet's childhood are seen to fade and vanish as "the shades of the prison-house" close round the boy. One by one his childhood's illusions are dissipated by matter-of-fact reality, by the "light of common day."

Riquet's dreams take form and substance in the person of Marguerite Charmaison, a young girl some years older than himself, who lives in Paris but pays occasional visits to the little town. Riquet adorned her with all the glories of his dreaming. He made her *la dépositaire attitrée de toutes les beautés du monde*. Margaret herself was filled with high aspirations and fervid longings. At fourteen she wanted to go on the stage. She admired Mounet-Sully, and carried in her pocket-book a frayed portrait of the great tragedian as Œdipus. This appalling picture she showed to Riquet to prove to him that it was art she adored and not the actor. Riquet listened and his admiration knew no bounds. Then Mounet-Sully faded from Marguerite's mind. Her father took her to Rome. There she met a young Englishman, Lord Wolseley, a disciple of Cardinal Newman. Wolseley inspired Marguerite with an adoration for the English Cardinal. He pointed him out to her as he said Mass in a chapel at St. Peter's; he presented her to him in the Pincio Gardens. Then on her return to France Marguerite received the announcement of Wolseley's death in a letter from the Cardinal himself. She showed that letter to Riquet as she had shown him Mounet-Sully's photograph.

In this fickle damsel's heart Newman's reign, curtailed possibly by the young lord's death, was as short-lived as Mounet-Sully's. Marguerite soon announced that she had discovered philosophy. She spent her days at the Sorbonne. She cited hideous German names. She translated Kant. She wrote *idea* with a capital I ; and she showed Riquet her Professor's photograph.

Each of these changes cut little Riquet to the heart. "Il y a toujours," he writes, "un sentiment de tristesse à apprendre que quelqu'un a changé d'idées."

Riquet's own little soul meanwhile was meditating on great things—*grandes choses*. What are great things, he was asking. Are they to recite verses as Marguerite used to do ? Are they to go to Rome and fall in love with a Cardinal ? Are they to feel God in the wind as it blows through the Courance pines ? Are they to be a motionless bronze statue like that of Alfred de Vigny on the square, or to die as Riquet's mother had died ?

For Marguerite "great things" had resolved themselves into a commonplace marriage with a commonplace husband. For Riquet there were moments when "great things" seemed to be the healing of his parents' feud with the most influential family of the town and their entering into possession of a long-coveted house. But once realized, these "great things" seemed to shrink to the dimensions of an ant-heap, and there remained something infinitely greater beyond. What was it? Did the bronze Alfred de Vigny see it from his pedestal on the square? What was he looking at? Did he see God or did he see nothing?

Little Riquet in contact with life had shed many of his illusions. Yet there still remained to him "obstinate questionings" and a dim vision of that immortal sea which brought him hither.

Riquet was happier than another of M. Boylesve's characters, Madeleine, the heroine of *La Jeune Fille bien Elevée.* In her case, the commonplace, in the form of a marriage of convenience, completely extinguished all her youthful ardour.

Madeleine was a born enthusiast. She

inherited this tendency from her father, who had lost his fortune in serving the Royalist cause. In the eyes of Madeleine's grandmother, Madame Coiffeteau, who dominated her family, much as *tante* Félicie did hers, Madeleine's father was a fool. And Madame Coiffeteau determined her daughter should avoid her father's folly. For Madame Coiffeteau the plan of life was laid out as regularly as a Dutch garden. A daughter must resemble her mother and regulate her life in precisely the same way. Madame Coiffeteau knew exactly the year when her granddaughter should go to boarding-school, when she should leave, when she should wear long frocks, when she should come out, and when she should marry.

Unfortunately Madeleine's enthusiasm from time to time threatened to disturb her grandmother's calculations. At her convent boarding-school she threw herself so heartily into religion that there was danger of her becoming a nun. She was adjured to be more moderate in her piety. She could not understand how one could be too religious. What about the saints ? she argued. The saints may be taken as models, she was told, but it would be presumptuous to endeavour to attain to their perfection. Then gradually in Madeleine's heart a more human passion succeeded religious devotion. A time came when, after the long holidays, she returned to the convent a different creature. She herself was barely conscious of the change, but the keen eyes of the nuns detected it. "There is some change in you; what has happened during the holidays?" asked one of the sisters. "Nothing," replied the girl. But the nun persisted. "Search in your own heart, my child." And thus pressed, terrified at this severe examination, the child replied, "Madame, perhaps it is that I am too much in love with Jesus Christ." That perspicacious nun was not deceived. She knew better than Madeleine herself what was happening in the young girl's heart. And after a time Madeleine herself realized that she had fallen in love at first sight with a certain René Chambrun, a young man who had turned over the pages for her as she played the piano at a friend's house one Sunday afternoon. For a year Madeleine treasured René's image in her heart. She idealized him as Riquet had idealized Marguerite Charmaison, as we all idealize the object of our youthful passion. She met him again. She was struck by the incongruity between her imaginings and the reality. But she still loved. Her unsolicited affection betrayed itself. Madame Coiffeteau was horrified. She read her granddaughter a severe lecture, and Madeleine was astounded by her grandmother's reproaches. She had sought to nourish in her heart a sentiment so grand, so exalted, "si conforme à ce que nous enseignaient la littérature, la musique, la religion même, qui est tout amour." Again she was puzzled. Was love like piety, a thing to be spoken of only in certain circumstances, a great passion, the examples of which were to be admired but not imitated?

Time effaced the image of M. René Chambrun from Madeleine's heart. Another enthusiasm possessed her. Now it was a passion for art, for music. But here again conventionality in the person of Madame Coiffeteau intervened to say to *la jeune fille bien elevée*, "thus far shalt thou go and no farther." Poor Madame Coiffeteau's notions of propriety received another rude shock when Madeleine was invited to play at a concert.

"Art, Art," she cried. "Upon my word, I don't understand what you are talking about. . . . I am certainly too old. . . . Last year it was love. His Majesty Love with a capital letter. . . . The year before, it was religious devotion. . . . I am bewildered. My parents lived to be much older than I am. They had seen many wars, tumults and revolutions. But I don't think they ever had to contend with such folly."

Moderation in all things, mistrust of *les sentiments exaltés*, this was the chief essential in a well-bred damsel.

In spite of all Madeleine's high aspirations she had finally to submit to a *mariage de convenance*. She strives against it up to a certain point. She boldly tells the suitor from Paris, M. Achille Serpe—our author is as happy as Dickens in his choice of expressive names—that though flattered by his attentions, her heart is a stone. This confession, however, misses its effect. It only serves to convince M. Serpe that Madeleine is what he most desires, *une jeune bien elevée.* Had Madeleine owned to being in love with him his sense of propriety would have been shocked. He had sought to marry a girl of perfect breeding, because, as Madeleine overhears him say on their wedding day, with such a wife he is sure of never being . . . And Madeleine obeys because her grandmother's training has borne fruit. She may rebel, but at a certain point she will always yield, for deep down in her subconsciousness there resides a certain conservatism, a certain respect for convention.

In the sequel to *La Jeune Fille bien Elevée*, in *Madeleine Jeune Femme*, we find this innate but subconscious sense of propriety enabling Madeleine married to resist a temptation much more seductive than any which had assailed her as *jeune fille*. In some of the most subtly psychological lines he has ever penned M. Boylesve tells of the great crisis in Madeleine's existence. She had received the declaration of M. Juillet, her would-be lover. She was happy and proud that it had been made. Her heart responded to M. Juillet's passion. And yet, at the same time and despite herself, there surged from the depths of her subconscious self such a strong sentiment of revolt against the irregularity of this proceeding that it effaced upon her countenance any expression of pleasure, it produced such a look of horror that M. Juillet, believing he had committed a deplorable blunder, turned away overcome by disappointment and remorse. But in his own words we must let M. Boylesve explain this delicate situation:

"Mais, en même temps, et d'une source étrangère à ma conscience, mais non pourtant étrangère à moi, monta tout le long de mon corps, m'environna, s'appliqua sur tous mes membres et sur mon visage, avec l'exactitude d'un linge mouillé, quelque chose comme une réplique de moi, quelque chose d'aussi moi que moi, et que, cependant, je repoussais comme mon propre fantôme aperçu, hostile, armé contre moi. Oh! cela n'avait rien de fantastique ni de surnaturel; c'était une attitude qu'adoptait mon corps tout entier, une attitude que je sentais saisie avidement par chacun de mes membres, par chacun de mes traits, et une attitude en contradiction flagrante avec mes sentiments véritables, une attitude de catastrophe, de malheur public, une attitude d'appel désespéré à toutes les énergies sociales et privées."

Here M. Boylesve goes down to the very foundations of social order. It is this subconscious "sense of fitness," as some would call it, or "adherence to convention," as by others it might be defined, which renders civilized society possible and its abuses tolerable.

Later in the book the author explains and accounts for this curious subconscious impulse. Madeleine, talking of this episode to an old school friend, Charlotte, who had been educated with her in the same convent, speaks of "la grande aile protectrice qui m'a sauvée de la faute et qui est quelque chose de bien plus auguste que moi, que ma volonté, que notre vertu, quelque chose fait d'un amoncellement d'honnêteté dans nos familles, quelque chose fait de la parole de nos communes maîtresses, dix ans écoutée et poussée plus loin même que notre esprit jusqu'à notre chaire, jusqu'aux muscles de notre visage; quelque chose d'un bien plus large et plus fécond enseignement que n'eût été ma résistance volontaire, isolée, chétive. . . ."[1]

[1] *Madeleine Jeune Femme*, pp. 355–6. "The great protecting wing which saved me from falling. It is something greater than I, than my will or our virtue. It is something which consists in the accumulation of goodness and honesty in our families, in the words of our common governesses, harkened to for ten years

"The inherited accumulation of goodness and honesty!" This idea approaches very near to Barrès' doctrine of faithfulness to the spirit of one's ancestors.[1] There is something Barrèsian, too, in the theory that the teaching of those Catholic nuns sank deep into the child's nature, penetrating into something more primitive than the intelligence—which, after all, cries Barrès, is but a little thing on the surface of ourselves—entering into the girl's very flesh and muscles and bearing fruit in after years in defiance even of the woman's own conscious will. One is not surprised to find Boylesve described as a disciple of Barrès; and the disciple is not unwilling to own to the master's influence. He, like Barrès, is a fervent advocate of social order and discipline. Like Barrès, too, though an agnostic, he has a tenderness for the Catholic Church. The portraits of priests in his novels he paints with a loving, reverent hand; and we suspect that he does not altogether disagree

and penetrating deeper than our minds, entering into our very flesh, into the muscles of our countenances. It is something far greater and more productive than could ever have been my own voluntary, isolated and weak resistance."

[1] See *ante*, p. 24.

with the Curé de Beaumont, when, in *L'Enfant à la Balustrade*, he makes him say of the Church's teaching, "even the unbeliever must admit that it is the result of the accumulated experience of centuries, and therefore more likely to meet the needs of men than any improvised system." Such a statement is allowed to pass unchallenged by the very obvious retort that the Church's teaching may be equally the result of the errors of centuries, and that at one period of Church history the Jew might have urged against the adoption of Christianity precisely the same argument as the Curé de Beaumont uses in its favour. But to such criticism our author would doubtless reply that he is writing a novel, not engaging in religious controversy.

Barrèsian as he may be, and to-day all the younger French writers are more or less under Barrès' influence, M. Boylesve is far from going the length of his master in pressing the claims of the Catholic Church. Indeed, it is not without misgiving that he sees the intellectual youth of present-day France turning churchwards.

Another feature which distinguished M.

Boylesve from many of the new French writers on the eve of the War is his irony. Irony was then falling into disrepute in France. That bright weapon of the French intellect, that trenchant sword of the spirit wielded so powerfully by French writers, from Voltaire to Anatole France, was too often being left to rust in the scabbard. How one longed for a gleam of it to temper the violent denunciations of M. Romain Rolland in *Jean Christophe.* But irony requires a certain aloofness and self-restraint which the new school of French writers pride themselves on not possessing. Their one concern is to plunge deep into the whirling stream of life and to allow themselves to be carried away by its current. They condemn the Ironists, whom they accuse of standing coldly on the bank gazing with a superior air on their comrades battling with life's billows. They accuse those Ironists of lacking comprehension and, above all, of lacking pity.[1] Even that King of Ironists, Voltaire, the greatest humanitarian in the most humanitarian of centuries, simply because he chose to produce emphasis

[1] See Victor Giraud, *Les Maîtres de l'Heure.* Chapter on Anatole France, p. 308.

by understatement, is charged with failing to comprehend and to pity. The author of this charge forgets or takes care not to mention Calas and Sirven and La Barre, and all those other persecuted and oppressed whose cause Voltaire so powerfully befriended. Pity, we are told, is inconsistent with irony. How comes it then that the greatest Ironists —one thinks at once of such names in our own literature as Swift and Defoe, Thackeray and Thirlwall—have always been the apostles of the oppressed and the exposers of social wrongs? Pity inconsistent with irony! Happily there is still with us to prove the gross fallacy of such a statement Voltaire's great descendant, who, in his *Jardin d'Epicure*, reminds us that Irony and Pity are both of good counsel. "Irony," writes Anatole France, "need be no cruel deity. She mocks neither love nor beauty. She is gentle and kindly disposed. Her mirth disarms anger; and it is she who teaches us to laugh at rogues and fools whom but for her we might be so weak as to hate."[1]

[1] *Le Jardin d'Epicure*, p. 122, in Mr. Alfred Allinson's translation.

For René Boylesve, as we have seen, life would be intolerable were it not for irony, which permits us to smile at the strange incongruities and contradictions of human existence. The spirit of irony penetrates all his work. It reveals itself not merely in the treatment of single episodes, but in the entire conception of certain novels, such as *Le Bel Avenir*, where he satirizes the pettiness and ineffectiveness of the average middle-class ambition, but more remarkably still does it permeate another novel, *Le Médecin des Dames de Néans*.

The Néans doctor had a patient, one Madame Durosay, beautiful and charming, whose case drove him to despair. Her malady was an incurable languor which prevented her from exerting herself or taking interest in anything. Suddenly there occurred to the doctor an idea, and the book might well have been entitled "the doctor's idea." It flashed upon him in all its brilliance as he sat in his study opposite a beautiful photograph of the Nikē and the inevitable Hippocrates bust surmounting a row of bound volumes of *La Gazette des Hôpitaux*. What was the idea? Simply this, that here was a beautiful young woman dying of languor, becoming too indolent even to desire pleasure. And why ? Because her marriage of convenience with a dull sod of a lawyer *a laissé vierge toute sa femininité.* The only possible cure is to make her fall in love. The victim is ready to hand in the youth Septime, a pupil of an excellent old Abbé, who with the doctor was a frequent visitor at the lawyer's house. Certain difficulties and moral scruples which present themselves, first in the person of the husband, then in that of the Abbé, the doctor speedily dismisses. After all he is not concerned with the moral order. His work is to save bodies, " de maintenir toutes les fonctions des corps et d'en dégager une belle harmonie."

And so he ruthlessly and successfully carries out his idea. Pitilessly the idea advances, passing cruelly, like the car of Juggernaut, over the body of the Abbé, who dies with horror at his pupil's sin, crushing also in its course the poor pupil himself, who drowns himself or attempts to drown himself—we are left in doubt as to whether the doctor who rescues him from the pond succeeds in restoring animation to his body—because another has superseded him in Madame Durosay's affection. And so skilfully is the plot constructed, that we are half in doubt as to whether the story is not being told in all seriousness, whether the author may not himself be of the doctor's way of thinking. Not until the last paragraph does the complete irony of the tale flash upon us in all its brilliance.

The doctor has brought Septime out of the pond. Leaning over the poor victim's body he sees Madame Durosay supported by the arm of her lover, Septime's rival. In the midst of his life-saving operations, the doctor murmurs to himself: "Ah! it's all right. Over there in the shade my idea is progressing, it's working of itself and more quickly than I ever dreamed."

The idea! how worthless, how cruel! How many such ideas does not the history of humanity reveal! Once they are conceived and put in practice, once they are started, then like a stone rolling down the mountain's side, they progress with increasing impetus, carrying everything before them. Such thoughts of profound philosophy, expressed with the clearness, the dignity and the restraint of classic French prose, now enlivened by gleams of merriment, now saddened by tears of pity, form the warp and woof of M. René Boylesve's work.

PIERRE MILLE

THE WORKS OF PIERRE MILLE

1897. De Thessalie en Crète.
1899. Au Congo Belge.
1903. Le Congo Léopoldien.
1905. L'Enfer du Congo.
Sur la Vaste Terre.
1906. Les deux Congo devant la Belgique.
1908. Barnavaux et quelques Femmes
L'Enfant et la Reine Morte.
Quand Panurge Resuscita.
1910. La Biche ecrasée.
1913. Paraboles et Diversions.
1914. Le Monarque

And "hundreds of tales," writes M. Mille, "which I, being the most negligent of men, have never collected into a volume."

PIERRE MILLE, 1865

AMONG the writers of French fiction on the eve of the War M. Pierre Mille ranks alike with the elder and with the younger generation. With the former his anti-clerical attitude and his ironical manner connect him, with the latter a love for distant travel, an interest in savage races and in the problems of colonization.

Of that Entente Cordiale, which for many years before the war existed not only in politics but in literature, Pierre Mille has been one of the most effectual inspirers. It was he who first introduced to French readers Rudyard Kipling and H. G. Wells. For the first of Mr. Wells's stories to appear in French, *The Stolen Bacillus*, M. Mille found an able translator in M. Achille Laurent.[1] M. Mille himself was the first Frenchman to translate

[1] At the hands of M. Henri Davray, who has since translated several of his novels into French, Mr. Wells has fared no less happily.

Kipling. It is now twenty-seven years ago since, returning to Paris from London, where he had been writing of an omnibus strike, he happened on a copy of *Many Inventions*. So completely was he captivated that he immediately translated two of its stories : *The Lost Legion* appeared in *le Temps*, *Matter of Fact* in *La Revue de Paris*. Thus was laid the foundation of that Kipling cult which was to prevail in twentieth-century France. Most of Kipling's works have now appeared in French. French children of to-day are brought up on " The Jungle Books." Some half dozen contemporary French novelists, among whom, in addition to Pierre Mille, the best known are Claude Farrère, Paul Adam, and Louis Bertrand, claim Kipling as their master. But this great English writer's influence extends far beyond the realm of pure literature. The spirit of his works has entered into French youth ; and Young France, as we see her to-day in the trenches, is developing characteristics which she first learnt to admire in the Anglo-Saxon heroes of Rudyard Kipling's tales.

Pierre Mille has himself been described as " the French Rudyard Kipling." The title is not altogether happy. M. Mille possesses far too much originality to be the imitator of any one. And he has himself said that it is impossible to imitate Kipling. Moreover, the temperaments of the two writers differ entirely in certain respects. While Kipling has ever believed in the ennobling influence of international warfare, M. Mille has always strenuously advocated international peace. While Kipling is too British to be anything but a member of the Church of England, Mille is too French to be anything but a pagan. Kipling is the greater artist of the two, for M. Mille is too much of a social reformer to be an artist pure and simple. In method also they differ. On this subject when, not long ago, Mr. Kipling visited Paris, he and M. Mille had an interesting conversation which was reproduced in *le Temps*.[1] Mr. Kipling seemed at a loss how to describe his methods. His stories, like Topsy, seemed just to grow. They were almost a product of his sub-consciousness. "The door is shut," he replied to M. Mille, who questioned him. "But you, how do *you* do it," he asked, turning the tables on his interrogator. M. Mille had no difficulty in replying. He,

[1] *Le Temps*, April 15, 1914.

unlike Kipling, is acutely conscious of his method of composition; and, with a Frenchman's lucidity, he described it: "It seems to me," he said, "that I begin with one little circumstance, which to any one else might appear trivial—with a face seen by chance but which has struck me—with a gesture as to the meaning of which I am curious. Then I reconstitute the whole story, just as Cuvier reconstituted the animal out of one of its fossil bones and the analogies it suggested. And, when it is finished, it appears to me inevitable." [1]

Such being the points of difference between the two writers what are the points of similarity? M. Mille would be the first to admit that he owes much to Kipling. The debt would seem mainly to consist in the easy colloquialism and vigorous directness of the dialogue, in the choice and sometimes in the treatment of a subject. M. Mille's great creation, Barnavaux, the French soldier in a regiment of territorial infantry, is nearly related to Mulvaney and Ortheris. M. Mille's Franco-African tales in the volumes *Louise et Barnavaux*, *Barnavaux et quelques Femmes*,

[1] *Le Temps*, April 15, 1914.

and *la Biche Ecrasée,* are told with that humour, touched with high seriousness, which is so characteristic of his English master's stories of Anglo-Indian life. M. Mille, too, has his animal tales. Some of the best are contained in the volume entitled *Paraboles et Diversions;* others, not yet collected, have appeared in the columns of *le Temps.* His one-volume story of two Parisian children, entitled *Caillou et Tili,* is not unrelated to *Wee Willie Winkie.*

"Only women understand children thoroughly," wrote Kipling in his introduction to *Wee Willie Winkie,* "but if a mere man keeps very quiet and humbles himself properly, and refrains from talking down to his superiors, children will sometimes be good to him and let him see what they think about the world." M. Mille adopted just that attitude towards Caillou, the little French boy of five who is the hero of *Two Little Parisians.* And Caillou does indeed reward his friend by letting him see what he thinks about the world.

Caillou is a little boy of five, the youngest of a large family. His mother, who is neither rich nor poor, may be seen at home, or in the Tuileries Gardens, ever accompanied by a big workbasketful of little trousers, little sailor coats, little skirts and bodices. And the somewhat indiscriminate adaptation of these garments to the members of her family, which economy dictates, leads to a sad tragedy in Caillou's career. Caillou was generally a happy child. But there came a time when black melancholy settled down upon him. For days he was either very naughty or wrapped in gloom. The doctor came and prescribed medicine, which Caillou obediently swallowed, but his melancholy continued. His mother could not make him out. "Do go and see him," she entreated his friend, the writer of the story :[1]

"'He loves you. . . . I think he has something on his mind which he doesn't know how to explain. Perhaps he will tell you, for it seems as if he wouldn't trust any of us now.' . . . I went to see friend Caillou. . . . He came to me with outstretched hands, his dear mouth held up to me for a kiss, his eyes bright, and his little heart full of loving trust. He was wearing a frock bequeathed to him by his sister Lucile. At first we spoke

[1] *Two Little Parisians.* (London : John Lane.) English edition, translated by Miss Drillien.

of serious topics, of things which interested us both, a dog friend of ours, a submarine which was wrecked the other day in the Tuileries pond, and a little girl. Then he said to me of his own accord, 'I'm so miserable, old chap.' I put my arm round him, just round his shoulders, so that he should feel I was treating him like a man of my own age. But he burst into tears, like any small urchin. . . . Really touched by this, I said, 'What is the matter, Caillou ? Come, tell me about it.' He was sobbing too much to answer. At last he said to me in a low voice, so that I could only just hear, 'All the week they dress me like this, with Lucile's clothes, and on Sundays they give me trousers and a jersey ! '

" 'Well, Caillou ? '

" 'Well ! ' said he, in another burst of tears, 'how can I tell if I am a boy or a girl ? What am I ? What am I ? ' "

The delicious humour and the deep pathos of this story runs through the whole of M. Mille's work. But nowhere does it appear to greater and more delicate advantage than in the volume of *Barnavaux et quelques Femmes*. One of these women is Marie-fait-en Fer, a poor French outcast lured away into Africa by white-slave traffickers. While something in this character suggests Maria, Choulette's mistress, in *Le Lys Rouge* of Anatole France, there is more to remind one of Kipling's "Ould Pummeloe" in the "Daughter of the Regiment."

With the insight and sympathy of "his big brother," as M. Mille modestly calls Kipling, he enters into the religious, or, as some would call it, the superstitious life of savage peoples. That he has studied it closely appears in several of his stories, notably in the tale of two Madagascar girls, Ramany and Kètaka, contained in the volume entitled *Sur la Vaste Terre*. In this story occurs one of M. Mille's most striking episodes, not unlike some of the Indian tales of magic related by Kipling. The Frenchman, Galliac, in conversation with Kétaka, mentions the conquest of the town, Tananarivo, by the French commanded by General Duchesne. Shaking her head, Kétaka replied:

"It was not General Duchesne who took Tananarivo. It was Kinoly, the dead ogre who strikes folk dead, he whom no one has seen, because when one has seen him, one is not any longer, one never lives again, unless one knows the magic herb, the herb which grows on ancient graves, which the sorcerers gather while they are dancing. . . . When the French came from the West, three nights following, he was heard to laugh in the sacred wood of Ambölnmenga. He has the manners of a crocodile. His laugh clacks against his teeth. Rajaralabry, my brother, who slept near the graves, hid his head in order not to see him. . . . The Kinoly came down. He went to meet the French, more than a hundred thousand of them had landed. White French, black French who came from Africa, yellow French, very ugly, who are called *Arabous* and who live without women. And they all climbed up with big guns on wheels, with mules and things to go up in the air, and great jars full of wine. They threw bridges over the rivers and cut through mountains for their iron wagons to pass through, and, lying in their canvas houses, they laughed when evening fell. The Kinoly arrived in the great plain. Grass was there and nothing but grass—no rice, no sugar-canes, no manioc. The humped oxen fled before the Shade-which-walketh-ever. And the Shade came to the first of the *miaramila*, to the first of the soldiers. The Shade's crocodile face could not be seen. It was hidden in a great *lamba*. Only its eyes were red like blood in a coal. It sneaked gently up to the soldiers, bending its head like a beggar. And the French *miaramila* said to him :

"'Beggar, your nails are very long!'

"The Kinoly spread out his claws and said :

"'They have grown in the earth.'

"Then he opened his *lamba*. And the French *miaramila* said :

"'Your belly is transparent!'

"'Because it has decayed in the earth.'

"And the *miaramila* said again :

"'Your eyes are very red.'

"Then the Kinoly took his shroud in his hands, threw it away, and said :

"'Look.'

"He had no eyes, but two holes with fire inside and dead flesh on the bones of his face.

"The soldiers all turned pale, fever seized them, and they died.

"The Kinoly came down again. He looked at the *Arabous*, he looked at the blue men whom you brought from the other side of Africa, the white officers in white uniforms. He walked in the midst of them, he wakened them at night, he startled them as they sat at meat, he laid his hand on their mules' bridles. And when they had seen the dead ghoul which brings death they turned pale and died. Some perished in the sand, some in the red earth, some in the river ; the Kinoly revelled in the noxious odour and played with the flies. . . . That lasted two moons and then all were dead.

"Then Kinoly went up to Tananarivo because he wanted to see Raini-laiarivony, the chief minister, the queen's husband.

"He found the aged minister asleep in his European palace in the midst of great luxury. And the Shade-which-walketh-ever struck him on the shoulder, bidding him awake.

"'I have stricken all the French with death,' said the Kinoly, 'now it is your turn. You are old, follow me willingly.'

"But the minister awoke without fear and looked at the Kinoly without dying, for he had the magic herb. Then the Kinoly, furious, went down into the plain where were all the French corpses. He touched them one by one with his finger, saying, 'Arise.' And they all rose. . . . The men took their guns, the officers drew their swords . . . and they marched up to Tananarivo. Then the chief minister said :

" 'The Shade lied to me, for here the devils come.'

" The Queen's soldiers were brave. But when they came up to the Frenchmen they turned grey with terror and their teeth chattered. For these were not men, these Frenchmen, they were Kinolys. They had no eyes, but holes filled with flame and their flesh hung green and decomposing on their bones. Their bellies were transparent, claws had they for fingers, and their jaws opened like the jaws of corpses when they are exhumed. They marched swiftly, swiftly, their feet made no noise, their guns gave out no smoke but killed like lightning. . . . The Queen's general Ramasombazana threw away his sword and his plumed helmet. The soldiers threw down their arms and fled. And the French corpses continued to advance, they climbed the hills, they descended into the valleys, walls crumbled to the ground when they touched them. . . . And the aged chief minister, who had married three queens, began to weep because the Kinoly had conquered.

"And he surrendered Tananarivo to the ghosts."

This vivid story, so typical of man's mind in its primitive, pre-civilization phase, recalls, as we have said, more than one episode in Mr. Kipling's work; and no one will hesitate to say that M. Mille is no sufferer from the comparison. The main theme of *Ramany et Kètaka*, however (the two little Madagascar girls who become the temporary wives of two Frenchmen), suggests rather Loti than Kipling, although it is not treated with quite the poetic tenderness of Loti's *Azyadé* and *Mme. Chrysanthème*.

Questioned as to the origin of the Kinoly tale M. Mille gave the following account of its inception: in the native folk-lore of Madagascar he found numerous stories of a hideous monster named Kinoly; to the natives' descriptions of this ghoulish creature he has remained absolutely faithful; but it was out of his own fertile imagination, fired by an English eye-witness's account of Tananarivo's capture by French soldiers, whom the ravages of climate, fatigue and disease had worn to mere shadows, that M. Mille evolved the episode of the taking of the town by Frenchmen, slain by the Kinoly's deadly glance, but brought back to life by him and transformed into Kinolys.

Questions raised during the last thirty years by the foundation and extension of a great French colonial empire occupy a prominent place in M. Mille's work, both in his tales and in the four volumes on the Congo which he contributed to *les Cahiers de la Quinzaine*, *Au Congo Belge* (1899), *Le Congo Léopoldien* (1903), *L'Enfer du Congo* (1905), *Les deux Congo devant la Belgique* (1906).

In fiction it is Barnavaux, sometimes a French soldier of marines, sometimes a private in a regiment of colonial infantry, whom his creator meets at Tonkin, in Madagascar, on the Congo, and in Paris, who generally raises these questions; and, from the discussion which ensues, one may conclude that Barnavaux's creator is very doubtful as to the benefits accruing to the coloured races from the white man's domination—that on the whole he is inclined to regard colonization as an evil, but an inevitable one.

Barnavaux, set to govern a district of Madagascar, cannot help pitying his native subjects even when they rebel ; for he sees internecine wars and insurrection against their white rulers, driving many of them from their homes. And when at length they are reduced to throw down their arms and return to their homesteads, what do they find there ? Nothing but poverty—their stores of rice vanished, their oxen stolen, and their corn-fields unsown. And what are the blessings they reap from the white man's government ? All those things which sound so fine when they figure in the governor's report printed in French newspapers—taxes on land, taxes on markets, taxes on cattle, compulsory labour.

Such are the reflections of Barnavaux. Nevertheless this French soldier is firmly convinced of the superiority of the white races and of their right to dominate over their coloured brethren. Any suggestion of intermarriage fills him with horror. He and the writer, coming out of a Paris metro' station, see a pretty French girl waiting for a little Jap who had been one of their fellow travellers. " She was not a duchess, for she came straight from the workroom, but she was attractive, ardent, and evidently much in love with that curt, disdainful Oriental. I," admits Pierre Mille, "felt angry and disgusted. A kind of impersonal jealousy came over me.

"'There it goes,' cried Barnavaux, furious, 'there it goes, the conquest has begun! They are capturing our women.'

"But I remarked rather sadly:

"'You needn't get so angry, Barnavaux. When we go to Japan, we too take the little *mousmés*.'

"'Yes,' retorted Barnavaux, naïvely, 'but it isn't the same thing; we are whites.'"[1]

Barnavaux thinks that the coloured races are best kept at home. They should not be encouraged to visit the white man in his native land for fear lest they should lose that veneration, which Barnavaux thinks is so salutary both for them and for us. It made him mad to see at the Paris Exhibition, in the Temple of Cambodge, a black soldier from Annam, keeping order among the white visitors. He resented being told to keep to the left by a coloured creature who did not even take the trouble to rise from his chair

[1] *Le Japonais* in *Barnavaux et quelques Femmes.*

when addressing this glorious marine in uniform. Only a second did Barnavaux, who had lunched and copiously, hesitate: then, picking the Annamite up by the collar, he sat down in his place, and, taking the dethroned official on his knee, kissed him on both cheeks.

In this tipsy French marine's brutality there lies a profound significance. And one wonders what will be the effect of the War on the Barnavaux not only of France but of England. Will life in the trenches, will a heroic resistance to a common foe help to humble this racial arrogance? If it should have this result, if it should make the whites realize that, despite the colour of their skin, the negroes and the Japanese are after all their brethren, then even this cruel War will not have been fought in vain.

Many other racial problems M. Mille touches upon in his stories. He raises, for example, the puzzling question, suggested by the Kikyu controversy, of the effect on the converted black man's mind of the strife and division among the various Christian sects and churches. For M. Mille, though a pagan, is very much occupied with Christianity. He is the disciple of Renan, the personal friend of Anatole France. Some of his best stories, *le Miracle*, for example, and *Comment le Déluge eut lieu en vain*,[1] are written in the true Anatolian vein. The irony of the Deluge story is delightful. Imagine the horror of Noah and his family regarding themselves as the sole survivors of the flood, and then coming out of the Ark only to be confronted by Deucalion and Pyrrha. Both patriarchs are equally furious. Each reproaches the other with not having been drowned. And then in a few suggestive lines M. Mille paints the contrast between the Hebraic and the Greek temperaments, between Noah's gloom and Deucalion's joy in living. But, to be appreciated, this story must be read.

M. Mille, *voyageur impénitent et passionné*, having wandered over the face of the earth, has now for some years fixed his abode in Paris. For, as he tells us, the Parisians, with the exception of Chinese Mandarins, are the only people in the world who have thoroughly acquired the art of politeness. But here we must ask leave to differ from our author and to include among Parisians and Chinese

[1] See *Paraboles et Diversions*.

Mandarins the natives of Choisy-le-Roi, where M. Mille first saw the light—for in no household, Parisian or Chinese, reigns truer politeness than in the beautiful home of M. Mille and his gifted wife,[1] on the quaint old quay in l'Ile de St. Louis, one of the most picturesque quarters of old Paris.

As he now lives in France, M. Mille in his last volume, *le Monarque*,[2] has written of France alone, and never has he produced anything more glittering with wit, with verve and with irony tempered by pity, than the tale which gives its title to this volume.

Like many other eminent characters of French fiction, notably *Crainquebille* and *Jean Christophe*, *le Monarque* made his first appearance in *les Cahiers de la Quinzaine*.[3] In the present volume M. Mille has considerably expanded and developed the slight sketch of six years ago. *Le Monarque* is the personification of *le démon du midi*. He descends from Sancho Panza, through the line of Tartarin de Tarascon and of Maurin des Maures.[4]

[1] Madame Mille, who is an eminent sculptor, is better known by her maiden name of Serruys.

[2] English edition, *Under the Tricolour*, translated by Miss Drillien.

[3] Ninth series, 1908.

[4] A novel by Jean Aicard. See *post*, pp. 288 *et seq*.

"It is time that we understood once and for all," wrote Daudet, "this reputation for lying from which *les méridonaux* suffer among the men of the North. There are no liars in *the midi,* no more at Marseilles than at Nîmes, no more at Toulouse than at Tarascon. The man of the South does not lie, he deceives himself. He does not always tell the truth, but he thinks he tells it. . . . His lying is not lying, it is a kind of mirage."

And so *le Monarque* lives and moves and has his being in a "mirage." He lives like a king, and why? "*Parce que je ne me f. . . rien,*" he explains to one of his friends. He is a hero, for does he not live in the land of heroes?

C'est une chose certaine mon cher, me dit Touloumès, qui parlait voluptueusement à travers sa pipe! la patrie de l'héroisme est ici. C'est prouvê depuis le temps des camisards.

And when *le Monarque* goes courting Madame Emma at Nîmes, when he tells her of his flocks and herds, his pastures and vineyards, "he lives a glorified existence, an existence magnified a hundredfold, a millionfold, grandiose." And the villagers of Espelmagne, who worship their monarch, help him to keep up the illusion. They fête him royally when he brings home his bride, and even she, when she discovers the deception, when she finds herself in a hovel instead of in a palace, cannot help admiring the magnificence of the mirage.

But the culmination of *le Monarque's* career is his heroic ride, his ride for a wager. He who had never for years bestridden a horse rides a hundred kilometres in a day and repeats it on the morrow. Such a ride! why it challenges comparison with all the famous rides of history and of literature, related both in prose and in verse.

It is strange that a writer, who in France has so long been the eloquent exponent of British thought and literature, should have remained comparatively unknown in this country. But the English version of M. Mille's tales, which is now appearing, no longer leaves English readers an excuse for such ignorance, especially as in his translator, Miss Berengère Drillien, M. Mille has found an interpreter who possesses at once the power of entering into her author's thought and of rendering it in fluent idiomatic English.

JEAN AICARD

THE WORKS OF JEAN AICARD

1867. Croyances.
1870. Au Clair de la Lune. (Play.)
1872. Pygmalion. (Play.)
1873. Mascarille. (Verses written for a Molière anniversary.)
1874. Poèmes de Provence.
Le Vénus de Milo. (A history of the statue's discovery according to unpublished documents.)
1876. La Chanson de l'Enfant.
1878. Poèmes de Provence. (Augmented edition.)
1879. Visite en Hollande.
Molière à Shakespeare. (Prologue in verse written to inaugurate the performances of La Comédie Française, at the Gaiety Theatre, London, translated into French.)
1880. Miette et Noré. (Poems.)
1882. Othello. (Translated from Shakespeare.)
1883. Lamartine. (A poem read by the author at a public meeting of the French Academy, November 15, 1883.)
1884. Smilis. (Play.)
1886. Le Livre des Petits.
1888. Au Bord du Désert. (Poem.)
1889. Don Juan. (Poem.)
Le Père Lebonnard. (Play.)
1890. Le Roi de la Camargue.
1893. L'Ibis Bleu.
1894. Fleurs d'Abîme.
1895. L'Eté à l'Ombre.
Diamant Noir.
1896. Notre Dame d'Amour.
Jésus. (Poem.)
1898. L'Âme d'un Enfant.
1904. La Légende du Cœur. (Play.)
1906. Benjamine.
1908. L'Illustre Maurin.
Maurin des Maures.
Le Manteau du Roi. (Play.)
1909. Discours, pronounced at his reception into the French Academy.

JEAN RICARD

JEAN AICARD, 1848

It may be objected that among French novelists of to-day Jean Aicard is out of place, that an author who was born in 1848, who was the protégé of Lamartine, the friend of Michelet, the correspondent of Flaubert and the disciple of Victor Hugo, belongs not to to-day, nor even to yesterday, but to the day before yesterday.

In a sense this is true. The spirit and the ideals which animated France in the middle of the last century animate Jean Aicard ; but they also animate Young France to-day. Yesterday is ever that period of the past which the present most completely ignores. Jean Aicard is more in touch with the French youth of to-day than many a writer who attained to the zenith of his influence at the opening of this century. Aicard and Young France resemble the grandfather, Jean Jacques Dailliot, and his grandson, Max, in Lichtenberger's last novel, *Le*

Sang Nouveau.[1] Max and his father had nothing in common; it required a grandparent to look at life from the young man's point of view. "The youth," writes Lichtenberger, "gazed at his grandfather with gratitude. Once again *leurs sensibilités se rejoignaient par-dessus la génération qui les séparait.*"

Though in the eighties Aicard was in his prime and enjoying considerable success, being crowned with national and academic honours, he remained true to the ideals of the previous generation and totally unaffected by those currents of science and criticism which were revolutionizing French thought and remoulding French literature. Zola's realism, Taine's intellectualism, Renan's scepticism, and the epicureanism of Anatole France all alike passed him by. Among realists Aicard remained an idealist (*obstiné dans son idéalisme*), among classicists a romanticist, among agnostics and atheists, if not a Christian, if not a deist, at least one "who regretted God" (*qui regrettait Dieu*).

Pierre Loti, when he received Aicard into

[1] See *ante*, p. 10.

the French Academy, aptly defined his religiosity as "the residuum of Christianity left in the human heart." Aicard himself describes his faith, now as "the religion of pity," now as "the religion of justice." But his pity is always Christian pity, his justice Christian justice, the religion

> qu'apporta Christ au vieux monde romain
> Et qu'appelle l'humanité lasse d'attendre.

How completely out of touch was Aicard with the spirit of the eighties appears in the unjust indictment he brings against it in his portraits of Lamartine and Michelet, whom he isolates from the age in which they lived.

"Both of them," he writes, "though of this century, belong to another period. Or rather, they belong to no age but to the eternal human. They are beings of faith and love, of elevation and tenderness. The aristocrat and the plebeian meet in the same grand, serene world, where all men are loved, where the slow but sure progress of justice is believed in. . . . Both, with the same exquisite delicacy, love women and children. No one more than they have spoken with reverence of the home, the family, 'the human nest lined with love.'

"They are beings for ever giving everything, even themselves.

"Now that impulse which is called sacrifice, generosity, blind self-forgetfulnesss, care for everything which founds a family for the country's sake and for everything which promotes the country's welfare for the world's sake, of that enthusiasm, the historical date of which is represented by the two figures 48—all that seems ended; it appears old-fashioned and a trifle absurd in this year of grace 1898.

"The note of the day is: personal and material interest. Sensation is everything, even in art and especially in literature. Why talk of sentiment? One earns money. One must earn money. Do you earn much money? Money, for your daily bread? No, for the purchase of sensations.

* * * *

"Woe unto them who in these days have Lamartine and Michelet for their masters. They will be the sanguine, the believers, at a time when, under penalty of death, mistrust in everything, disbelief in everything are required from us all.

*   *   *   *

"Alas! misled by those noble teachers, we dared to believe in the nobility of the human soul . . . and we continue to believe even when faith has deserted the majority of our fellow men. . . . The true cause of our despair is our tacit conclusion that, confronted by the infinite and its appalling silence, human effort is vain. . . . It only remains, we think, for us to establish ourselves in comfort on the earth, even though that comfort involve the massacring of weaker neighbours who stand in our way."

Aicard loves to pose as the apostle of justice; but in this passage he himself is unjust; for he completely ignores the immense impulse given to human effort by the critical examination of ancient beliefs and by scientific inquiry. Science and criticism have revealed that poverty far from resulting from any divine ordinance proceeds frequently from man's greed and misdoing. Science and criticism, by proving that we need not always have the poor with us, have given rise to that crusade against poverty which is one of the most encouraging signs of the present day. The growing discontent of the poor man with his lot Aicard regards as a misfortune. In his poem *La Révolte* he accuses the critic and the scientist of depriving the poor of their God, and thereby taking from them any inducement to bear their misery with resignation. He grieves to find that

> Le déchu se relève et somme
> Les riches et les triomphants,

Aicard is one of those well-to-do who deplore the poor man's discontent. Others thank heaven for the dissatisfaction of their less prosperous brethren, who have too long borne their suffering in silence.

It is not, however, as a philosopher or as a teacher of religion, but as a poet, both in prose and in verse, that M. Aicard occupies a place by no means insignificant among French writers of to-day. He and M. Richepin were chosen by the French Academy to reply to Mr. Rudyard Kipling's eloquent verses written on the occasion of M. Poincaré's visit to London in the summer of 1913.

In the following lines M. Aicard advocated that armed peace which the recent disclosure of Germany's designs proves to have been only too necessary.

> l'idéal guerrier de Jeanne, c'est le notre,
> Mais elle se voulait libre dans son pays
> Telle est Jeanne, Kipling ; elle est la Paix en armes.
> Elle, c'est nous ; ses vœux ne seront point trahis ;
> Voilâ pourquoi, rien en la nommant, tu nous charme.

Jean Aicard is a Provençal : he was born at Toulon. And Provence is the great inspirer of all his best work, whether prose or verse, lyric or epic poetry, the drama or the novel. Provence is for Aicard what Lorraine is for Barrès and Touraine for René Boylesve. What would French literature be without its Provençal writers, without the songs of the troubadours, the stories of Daudet, the poems of Mistral, and the novels of Aicard ?

Born and bred in Provence, there Aicard has continued to spend most of his days. Unlike Daudet and many another *méridional* he has never forsaken Provence for Paris. Whenever he does visit the capital, he never fails to rejoice as the time approaches for his return to his beloved *midi*. "Il lui suffit de toucher la terre maternelle," writes his biographer,[1] "et de respirer l'air du large pour refaire ses forces et renouveler son inspiration."

Among his fellow *provençaux* Jean Aicard is idolized. They have elected him for their bard; and everywhere—in the fisherman's cabin, in the woodlander's hut, as well as in the duke's mansion—he is welcomed with delight. The hunter, when he sallies forth in the morning, carries with him in his game-bag a novel by Jean Aicard; and in remote hamlets, during the long winter evenings, peasants gather round the children as they recite Aicard's poems learnt at school.

No wonder that Provençaux love this writer, for his work glows with Provençal sunshine, sparkles with Provençal fun, rings with Provençal laughter. Through his breezy pages blow the soft pine-scented zephyrs of Provence and the fresh wind from the Mediterranean. As Sully Prudhomme sang on the appearance of a volume of Aicard's verse,

> Tu nous a apporté de ton pays natal
> Ce qui nous manque ici l'air, le jour et la flamme.

[1] J. Calvet, *La Poésie de Jean Aicard*, p. 14.

The happiest moments of Aicard's childhood, he tells us, were spent in the open air. All nature seemed to him "one big person," whom he felt to be kind as long as daylight lasted. "How well I remember," he writes, "affectionately embracing an almond-tree's wrinkled trunk. I talked to it, and some of its delicate, fragrant pink blossoms fell on to my black-haired little head. Thus the tree replied to me." [1]

Too soon, alas! for this romantic, nature-loving boy came the time when the walls of the prison-house, in other words, of the *lycée*, closed in upon him. At the *lycée* of Maçon, he felt himself an exile, and not even pleasant outings to the château of his father's friend, the poet Lamartine, could reconcile this child of the South to banishment from his parents and from gay Provence. M. de Lamartine did his best to console the lonely boy.

But, wrote Aicard in after years:

> . . . ni le châtelain, dont je savais la gloire,
> Ni les dames m'offrant les gâteaux et le miel,
> Ni tant d'amis nouveaux n'effacèrent ton ciel,
> Provence, de mon cœur tout plein de ta mémoire.

[1] *L'Âme d'un Enfant.*

His hot Provençal blood did not tend to make the young Aicard a docile pupil. Like Daudet and like Mistral, he was not on the best of terms with his schoolmasters. More than one tussle between teacher and taught is recorded. Once he was reprimanded because in a letter thanking the great Lamartine for his hospitality, the *lycéen* had sent his compliments first to a favourite greyhound and afterwards to his hostess. This order of precedence was very characteristic of one in whose heart there has ever been a warm place for the weak and the helpless, for animals and for little children. Another schoolmaster's grievance was Aicard's passion for versifying—most unseemly it was thought in a school-boy, especially when the verses—as in Aicard's case—were published. Bidden to the headmaster's presence he was ordered to cease his literary labours. But soon his day of vengeance came. He was now at the *lycée* of Nîmes ; and the Bishop of Nîmes was to visit the school. Again Aicard was summoned to the headmaster's presence, this time to be addressed as *monsieur*, and to be politely requested to resume the forbidden pen in honour of the forthcoming visit. The prohibition once removed, Aicard revelled in writing verse and filled many volumes with his lisping numbers.

But the most glorious moments of these years were the holidays spent at Toulon with his grandfather, whom he adored, and to whose influence he has ever been proud to ascribe all that is best in his work :

Grand-père, tout cela, quelle qu'en soit la gloire,
Je l'ai pris à toi-même, à ta simplicité,
Au vieux air que tu m'as, le soir, cent fois chanté,
Au ton dont tu disais ta plus naïve histoire.

Je l'ai pris dans tes bras, dans ton cœur, dans ta main,
Dans l'oubli des cités où sont les choses laides,
Dans la vieille maison, seule au fond des pinèdes,
Et dont je ne veux oublier le chemin.

Tu fis mon œuvre simple, et ma voix attendrie,
Et je rapporte à toi ce qui vient de toi seul.

In a page of personal recollections Aicard describes his first arrival at his grandfather's house :

"We entered the garden . . . a garden conquered from the rock. Flowers watered at the cost of much labour, for the well was far away. Orange-trees all along the façade. Two Japanese mulberry-trees, which my

Uncle pointed out to me. Delightful garden-walks. Garden tools in a corner.

"We turned round. Now the doorway framed a picture of the distant sea, islands and ships, like a glimpse of fairyland. . . . Then my grandfather came and stood in front of me. He seemed to me very tall, although really of medium height, with broad shoulders and the chest of an athlete.

"'Listen,' he said, 'I want you to be happy here. Everything in my house is yours. First this: the view of the sea, of the forests and of the sky, which God gives you. . . . The wealthiest people in the world, kings and princes, come to our country in order to possess this beautiful sight. But they are compelled to go away, because they must live their lives elsewhere. All this is ours, it is our country, it belongs to us. Enjoy it every day and love it. It deserves your affection.'"

His grandfather's injunction Jean Aicard has faithfully obeyed. With all his heart he has loved that beautiful country, and with an artist's pen he has painted its glories for those whom a less favourable fate has prevented from journeying thither. It was in verse that Aicard's passion for Provence first expressed itself ; and his poems early received recognition. Some of his youthful verses, which had been sent to Victor Hugo at Guernsey, were acknowledged in a letter which closed with the rhetorical sentence : "Aimez passionnément la vérité, la justice et la liberté . . . et aimez-moi un peu." Henceforth Hugo was his master, and the elder poet never lost interest in his disciple. "I promise this poet to France," said Hugo, when, at the height of his fame, departing from his usual practice, he came to the Academy to vote for the awarding of the prize Vitet to Aicard's poem, *Miette et Noré*. The young poet had the good fortune to belong to a literary circle. His father, who had died when he was but a child, had been a well-known author. His literary associations as well as his talent may have induced the Academy to look favourably on his work and to crown his second and third volumes of poetry, *Poèmes de Provence* and *La Chanson d'un Enfant*.

It was not until 1890 that Aicard published his first prose work, a novel, *Le Roi de la Camargue*, the first of a long series of novels, with all of which it is impossible to deal in this chapter. Some of them are rendered a trifle wearisome by the author's perpetual indulgence in moral reflections which break the thread of the narrative. One of them, *L'Âme d'un Enfant*, is a charming study of child life based on the author's recollections of his own childhood. But the novels by which Aicard will most likely live are those which portray the soul of Provence, *Le Roi de la Camargue*, *Maurin des Maures*, and *L'Illustre Maurin*. Provence plays some part in all Aicard's novels ; but these three books more especially are aglow with the Provençal spirit. How well it is portrayed with its rippling laughter, its twinkling mischief and its merry sarcasm, yet with its sky now and again overcast by clouds of passion, hatred and revenge! Nowhere in the world are jokes more appreciated than in Provence. And the peculiar form of Provençal joke is the *galejado*. What precisely is the *galejado? Tartarin de Tarascon*, for example, is one long *galejado* or series of *galejados*. Aicard defines it as a good-humoured joke, " a thing so wild that at first it sounds like an absurdity, yet containing just a point of sarcasm, just a flash of insight, which in spite of himself makes the victim exclaim: 'Why, yes! that is I! I am like that, and what's the harm?' Thus the President of a certain Provençal *Parlement*, the members of which were not distinguished for intelligence, brought home to them their stupidity. From his window he fired at a donkey: the donkey died; there was a law-suit. But the President, rising in court, said gravely: 'Gentlemen of the *Parlement*, I maintain that you are incompetent to judge this case, being all more or less related to the victim.'"[1]

The ass is a favourite subject of the *galejado*. Aicard's hero, Maurin, is a famous *galegeaire*. In one of his escapades he gets into trouble with the people of Gonfaron, a village, the inhabitants of which are renowned for their credulity; they will swallow anything, even the prevailing tradition that asses will fly. The whole village is pursuing Maurin, when he, in his flight through the forest, comes on a donkey browsing at the foot of a tree, to which she is attached by

[1] See Jean Aicard on "La Provence Joyeuse" in *Le Journal du Var*, and in his preface to Durandy's *Poussières du Midi*.

a cord. Now, says Maurin to himself, they shall see donkeys fly; and hoisting the innocent Nellie into the tree, he suspends her therefrom by the cord well hidden in the branches, and, affixing to the creature's back two pairs of partridge's wings, which he chanced to have in his game-bag, the fugitive makes off. The Gonfaronnais arrive, and, as Maurin expected, they fall into the trap; the marvellous spectacle arrests their pursuit; at first this fulfilment of tradition strikes them dumb with amazement. Some one wonders, however, whether there be not a trick in it. "Surely the wings are very small," exclaims one, "and not quite in the right position," ejaculates another. "Yes, but," retorts a pious Gonfaronnais, "angels in churches always have wings like that." And while they wonder, Maurin escapes.

Another favourite subject of the *galejado*, so Aicard tells us, is the top-hat. This pompous head-dress inevitably provokes laughter in Provence. By those who play the popular Provençal game of bowls it is worn merely to excite merriment; and this it never fails to do, for peals of laughter greet the ridiculous sight of a player, bowl in one hand and with the other vainly endeavouring to steady his headgear, which is generally of antique shape, having probably been borrowed from a grandfather's wardrobe. In one of the old Provençal mysteries of the Nativity, writes Aicard, which was played at a marionette theatre not long ago, one of the characters was a blind old man, who was led to the manger in the hope of recovering his sight. His guide, a boy of twelve, to honour the Holy Infant, had put on a high hat. When the time came for the man, kneeling before the Child Jesus, to announce the recovery of his sight, he proved it conclusively by turning to his guide with the exclamation : " *Mon Dieu*, what a hat ! "

For the scene of his Provençal novels Aicard has chosen two strips of coast, the Plain of La Camargue and the mountains of Les Maures ; and he has selected them because here, more even than in other parts of Provence, ancient customs linger and primitive conditions persist.

In another notable French novel of to-day, *Le Jardin de Bérénice*, Maurice Barrès has described the vast Camargue Plain, dotted here and there by shallow salt-water pools and intersected by canals. Over these low-lying flats roam the bulls which are kept for the bull-fights at Nîmes, at Arles, and at Avignon. Herdsmen or *gardians*, armed with lances and riding on fleet Provençal horses, exercise a somewhat desultory supervision over these fiery monsters. A time comes, however, when the *gardians* are compelled to shake off their Provençal lethargy: forming themselves into a semicircle round the bull they drive him to the town where the bull-fight is to take place. And the passing of the bull through Provençal villages by night Aicard describes in some of his most graphic pages.

One of these *gardians*, Renaud, known as *le Roi de la Camargue*, is the hero of Aicard's first novel. And the book tells of the conflict in his breast between vice and virtue, between love and lust. Vice and lust are represented by the gipsy queen, Zinzara, who bewitches the hero by her dark beauty, and wins him to be unfaithful to his betrothed, the pure, gentle Livette. In the end love and virtue conquer, but it is only through Livette's death. Renaud never forgives himself for his treachery: "If ever an hour of peace came to him, it was one morning, when in the midst of the nightmare which haunted him with the memory of Zinzara, Livette appeared, smiling, clothed in white, bearing lilies in her hand, like the saints in church windows, and saying to him: 'I have forgiven thee, forgive thyself.'" This novel of Provençal passion is full of powerful, vivid scenes: such, for example, as when Zinzara, like some malevolent dark-hued Venus, rises from the waves in superb nudity and, advancing, clings to Renaud's stirrup as he rides upon the shore and charms him; and again when Renaud rides with Zinzara to the lonely cabin in the marshes.

It is the passionate, the intense side of Provençal nature which is represented in this book. A more comprehensive picture of the Provençal temperament in all its moods, changing rapidly like an April sky from the dark clouds of hatred and revenge to gleams of sunny laughter and mischievous fun, is presented in the two Maurin volumes. These perhaps are the most widely known of Aicard's novels. They have been translated into English and into German.

The hero of these two volumes, Maurin

des Maures, l'Illustre Maurin, is, without exaggeration, one of the most fascinating characters of contemporary French fiction. He is the idealized personification of the Provençal temperament ; and as such he inevitably challenges comparison with Daudet's Tartarin de Tarascon. But, as one of Aicard's biographers [1] has pointed out, the two characters differ widely. "Tartarin is a masterpiece of caricature ; Maurin is the presentment of an ideal. Tartarin is swollen with pride. All his actions are inspired by vanity ; he is always ridiculous, and he is generally stupid. Maurin is too intelligent to permit himself to appear absurd. Deep-seated in his heart is a vague ideal of justice, to which he is ever faithful. He suggests Don Quixote, but a modern Don Quixote, who is witty, republican, and a freethinker, though nominally a Christian. There may be many Tartarins in Provence, but it would not do to say so. There may be only a few Maurins, but one must always say that there are many."

Maurin is not unrelated to our own picaresque heroes—to Tristram Shandy and to

[1] J. Calvet in *La Poésie de Jean Aicard*, p. 27.

Roderick Random. He is a character in whom Robert Louis Stevenson would have delighted, a true descendant of our Robin Hood and of his cousin, the French Robin du Bois. He is a hero of the greenwood, an outlaw, a poacher, who spends his days dodging *gens d'armes*, and, in the company of his faithful Little John, Parbo-Soulet, scouring the country-side, getting into every possible kind of scrape and making friends with every one, even with those who should have been his worst enemies, the landed proprietors, whose game he makes a profession of stealing.

In Maurin's blood there is an Arab streak, inherited from remote Saracen ancestors who, in the dimness of the dark ages, overran that part of France. And the Arab ancestry reveals itself in his Oriental manner of treating women. For this latter-day Robin Hood there is not one Maid Marian but many. He is the Don Juan of the woods, making love to all the pretty girls, not one of whom is proof against his blandishments. But, alas! for Maurin, one of these damsels happens to be a Corsican; and she takes Maurin's caresses too seriously, demanding that he shall be hers alone. This request, the hero, with a frankness which is one of his greatest charms, refuses; and the refusal ends in Maurin's death.

It is not, however, until he has entertained his readers with some eight hundred pages of Maurin's adventures that Aicard can bring himself to slay his hero; and ever since, so he tells us, he has bitterly regretted the event.

Maurin's passing is described in our author's most lyrical and impassioned manner. Here the fiction of the day before yesterday merges into that of to-day. For, if a paragraph may be likened to a chapter, Maurin's apotheosis is almost as sublime as that of the present-day hero, Romain Rolland's Jean Christophe.

Aicard's prose is throughout the prose of a poet and of a Provençal poet. Vivid facile, fluent, he is *l'âme chantante de Provence*, expressing ever in novel, poem, and play the spirit of that gay land.

As a dramatist Aicard has achieved considerable success. His play, *Le Père Lebonnard*, has been translated into several languages, and in its native tongue ranks as a classic. At the performance of another of his plays, *La Légende du Cœur*, in the ancient theatre of Orange, with Sarah Bernhardt playing the hero's part, Aicard received a magnificent ovation from ten thousand Provençaux, who made the old ruins resound with their applause. "Such a scene," said Loti in his *Discours de Réception*, "would have stirred your aged grandfather's heart even more profoundly than the welcome you receive to-day beneath the Academy's cupola."

INDEX

Index

Index

Index